The
Accelerated
Learning
Handbook

The Accelerated Learning Handbook

A Creative Guide to Designing and Delivering Faster, More Effective Training Programs

by Dave Meier

McGraw-Hill

New York San Francisco Washington, D.C. Auckland Bogotá
Caracas   Lisbon London Madrid Mexico City Milan
Montreal   New Delhi San Juan Singapore
Sydney Tokyo Toronto

McGraw-Hill

A Division of The **McGraw·Hill** Companies

1 2 3 4 5 6 7 8 9 0   AGM/AGM   0 9 8 7 6 5 4 3 2 1 0

ISBN 0-07-135547-2

The sponsoring editor for this book was Richard Narramore, the editing supervisor was Janice Race, and the production supervisor was Peter McCurdy. It was set in Sabon Roman and Akzidenz Grotesk.

Printed and bound by Quebecor World/Martinsburg.

Part 1: The Learning Revolution

Part 2: Natural Learning

Part 3: The Four Phases of Learning

Part 4: Additional A.L. Tools and Techniques

Part 5: Computers and Accelerated Learning

Part 6: Rapid Instructional Design (RID)

Part 7: The Learning Revolution and You

Resources: Literature, Music, Organizations

An Accelerated Learning Parable
From The Real World

Here's a story that will help you catch the spirit of Accelerated Learning (A.L.) right from the start. You'll encounter this same story later on. But it's presented here for those who want an instant grasp of some of the major ideas presented in this book.

It was 9 a.m. on a sunny Friday morning in Albuquerque. And it was the third and final day of a three-day A.L. workshop for 26 trainers at a major US semiconductor manufacturer. The phone in the training room rang. It was an emergency call for David, one of the participants. David took the call, hastily hung up, and told us that he would have to leave the class for an hour and a half.

He explained that this was the final day of a one-week orientation program for new hires going on in another building on site. An hour-and-a-half presentation on safety was scheduled for that morning. The person who was to teach it had to cancel. So David, who had taught it, was being tapped– and off he went.

Rushing to the other location, it dawned on him that he didn't have his presentation materials and handouts. What was he to do? Then he recalled one of the principles of the A.L. workshop he was in, namely that *learning is creation, not consumption.* "That's it!", he thought. He immediately had his plan.

Walking into the training room, he found the learners in an advanced and nearly terminal comatose state, having sat all week long while one subject matter expert after the other inundated them with a glut of information.

To bring them back to life, David immediately asked them to stand up, count off in fours, and form four teams. Then he gave them their instructions. The teams were to fan out into the organization for 20 minutes to find out as much as they could about safety in the organization. They were asked to encounter existing employees, explain their mission and ask them questions like, "What are the most important safety tips you can give us? What do we really have to watch out for when we're fabricating semiconductors in the plant? What's the worst thing that could happen to us in the factory?" He told them to get as much information as they could in 20 minutes and bring their findings back to share with the whole class. The teams then left in their quest for knowledge.

Twenty minutes later they were back – animated, excited, and definitely out of the comatose state. As each team reported their findings to the group, David had to do very little, other than to draw them out with a question now and then. To his amazement and delight, the learners were covering everything he would have covered, but in a far more effective way. And it didn't take an hour and a half. In just 50 minutes they had covered the material.

David got a big round of applause from the class. And they told him— now listen to this— that *this was the best presentation they had had all week!*

This true story illustrates beautifully some of the major principles of accelerated learning that you'll find in this book, namely:

1. Total learner involvement enhances learning.

2. Learning is not the passive storage of information but the active creation of knowledge.

3. Collaboration among learners greatly enhances learning.

4. Activity-centered learning events are often superior to presentation-centered ones.

5. Activity-centered learning events can be designed in a fraction of the time it takes to design presentation-centered ones.

A Special Note to Training Professionals

Here are a couple of suggestions that will help you get the most out of applying Accelerated Learning (A.L.) to your organization's training needs.

Don't Confuse A.L. With Fluff

Accelerated Learning has one aim only: to get results. You really have to distinguish it from those fun-and-games, gimmicky, "creative" approaches that call attention to themselves and are often a big waste of time.

The credo of the A.L. approach is "Do what works, and keep searching for what works better." It is not tied to any specific set of techniques, methods, or media– be they old or new, but can use any or all of them in combination, depending on their ability to deliver exceptional results.

It's important for you to understand that A.L. parts company with training approaches that attempt to be clever, cute, and fun for their own sake. By the same token, it parts company with training approaches that are inflexible, stoical, overly serious, and joyless for their own sake. There is a place for fun and a place for seriousness. We need both. And A.L. seeks to blend both in ways that enhance learning and produce the most positive outcomes possible.

Leading-Edge Learning

Accelerated Learning is the most advanced learning approach in use today, and it has many advantages. It is based on the latest research on the brain and learning. It can use a wide variety of methods and media. It is open and flexible. It gets learners totally involved. It appeals to all learning styles. It energizes and rehumanizes the learning process. It seeks to make learning enjoyable. And it is solidly committed to results, results, results.

A.L. methods are not set in stone, but can vary greatly depending on the organization, the subject matter, and the learners themselves. We believe, with the educational writer

Jacques Barzun, that "teaching is not the application of a system; it is an exercise in perpetual discretion." What matters most, after all, is not the method but the outcome.

A Proven Approach

Hundreds of organizations are using A.L. approaches today, and the number is growing steadily as more and more training professionals discover to their delight that they can:

- Design programs much faster
- Improve measurable learning
- Foster more creative, productive employees
- Save tons of time and money for their organizations

For example:

II Stanley quickly designed an upgrade for its soldering program that emphasized team-based immersion in "the real world." The course was reduced from 20 hours to 8, with a 30% improvement in measurable learning.

A major North American retailer using A.L. methods reduced a management class in coaching from two days to four hours by having managers help each other create their own coaching model and apply it to the job. Ninety percent of the participants reported a measurable improvement in their management skills. That never happened with the two-day non-A.L. course.

There are many more examples of A.L. successes in the section of this introduction titled *The Power of Accelerated Learning*. Check it out. The whole point is that **this stuff works**, and it works without trivializing the learners on the one hand or stressing them out on the other.

You Need Two Wings to Fly

To be totally successful with A.L., you've got to fly with the two wings of **skepticism** and **openness**. Yes, you need them both. Try getting anywhere with just one of those wings exclusively, and what happens? You fly in ever decreasing circles and eventually— thud!— you crash. But use them both in tandem and you soar. Sometimes we favor one wing over the other, or we fail to use both of them sufficiently to get us off the fence we're perched on. Then we go nowhere fast in fulfilling our roles as learning leaders.

Be Skeptical

There is so much educational junk food, fluff, and snake oil out there today, that you owe it to yourself and your organization to be skeptical. Based on my 30+ years of experience in the field, I've concluded that there is often not too much skepticism in training management, but not enough. Too often we fall prey to every new training "innovation" that comes down the pike without batting an eye.

Sometimes we rush to the latest technological panacea without first rethinking our assumptions about learning itself. Or we get dazzled by methods that emphasize "fun and games," clever gimmicks, and cutesy techniques without a shred of evidence that these things produce any lasting value.

It pays to be skeptical. Without discernment you can end up spending mountains of time and tons of money on learning approaches that trivialize the learner and the learning process and produce little or no long-term benefit.

Be Open

While exercising healthy skepticism, it's also essential to stay open to innovations that can result in genuine payoffs.

Life is a continual process of movement and change and growth. When we start to think that we've seen it all and heard it all, it's a danger sign. The only people who have truly seen it all and heard it all are the dead. For the living, life is always open to unending possibilities. And there are new possibilities knocking on your door all the time if you're open to them.

The universe and we ourselves are in constant flux. Nothing alive is dormant but is continually evolving. Just because a new way of thinking or doing things departs from your company culture, or what you've been conditioned to, this does not mean it's bad. Nor does it mean it's good. But when you keep searching for the good in the flux of life, separating the wheat from the chaff, you stay healthy, viable, and alive— mentally, spiritually, and professionally.

By exercising the two wings of skepticism and openness (in balance), you will be more able to distinguish the artificial from the real, find better ways to genuinely optimize learning, and enjoy greater success in your work.

A New Approach for The Learning Age

Today we desperately need to update our approaches to learning to meet the demands of our high metabolism culture. And the changes we need to make are not cosmetic but systemic, not mechanistic but organic.

Conventional learning methods, born in an early industrial economy, tended to take on a factory look and feel: mechanization, standardization, external control, one-size-fits-all, behavioristic conditioning (the carrot and the stick), fragmentation, and an emphasis on an "I-tell-you-listen" format (also known as the *Pour and Snore* technique). It was the only way, we felt, to prepare workers for the dreary, repetitive life of industrial-type work.

But now, training is no longer a matter of preparing docile, obedient factory workers, but knowledge workers who have to constantly absorb and adjust to new information. Now training's goal is not to teach people instinctual responses for relatively mindless assembly-line jobs, but to ignite people's full mental and psychological powers for thinking, problem solving, innovating, and learning.

Training for *The Learning Age* is characterized by total learner involvement, genuine collaboration, variety and diversity in learning methods, internal (rather than mere external) motivation, a sense of joy and excitement in learning, and a more thorough integration of learning into the whole of organizational life. The reason? Learning is no longer preparation for the job, it **is** the job.

The survival and health of individuals and organizations today depends on their ability to learn. And to learn not prescribed, repetitive behaviors, but how to think, question, explore, create, and constantly grow.

Since we're now in a *learning* culture like never before in history, finding ways to accelerate and optimize learning is paramount.

This Book's Intent

It is not the intent of this book to cover everything that could be said about accelerated learning and all the developments associated with it over the past 25 years. You'll find, for instance, no discussion of Gardner's theory of multiple intelligences, a topic that has been covered widely and more than sufficiently by other writers. Nor will you find a detailed account of the original language training methodologies of Suggestopedia (which, according to some, jump started the whole accelerated learning movement).

This book has a very focused mission: It wants to get to the heart of things and enable you to apply accelerated learning principles and methods to specific learning programs as quickly as you can, as widely as you can, and as often as you can. And it wants to give you enough solid grounding in the "why" so you can accomplish this with intelligence, grace, ongoing creativity, and assured success.

And so this book has been written not as an academic treatise but as a springboard to practical and immediate action. It's not intended for dilettantes but for front line practitioners of accelerated learning who want to venture forth and make substantial contributions to learning in today's world. Assuming this is you, hold on to this book. It will provide you with inspiration and ideas for fulfilling your vocation, achieving astonishing results, and enjoying your work like never before.

Learning is no longer preparation for the job, it **is** the job.

What Accelerated Learning Can Do For You

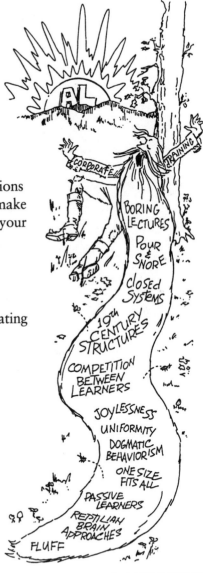

The Aim of This Book

This book has one major aim: to contribute to your pleasure and competence as a learning facilitator.

The book wants to move you beyond today's assumptions about learning into a fresh understanding that is bound to make you more creative, more energized, and more successful in your work.

Here's a broad-brush summary of what's in this book.

- Accelerated learning philosophies and principles.

- Hundreds of ideas, tips, and techniques for accelerating and enhancing learning.

- Concrete examples of A.L. in action.

- A systematic view of the human learning process.

- A time-saving rapid design method.

- Ideas for enhancing technology-driven learning.

- Resources to help you in your work.

The Wise Use of This Book

There are hundreds of ideas and techniques in this book that will help you. But more than that, it's the A.L. (accelerated learning) philosophy that will really get you going.

It's important for you to understand that A.L. is not intended to be a disjointed collection of clever tricks, gimmicks, and

It's a new day for learning, and time for a shave.

techniques, but a total system for speeding and enhancing both the design and the learning processes.

To simply implement the book's techniques without understanding the philosophy and principles underlying them will give you some success, but it will tend to be shallow and short-lived. However, by first understanding the A.L. philosophy and *then* implementing the appropriate techniques, you will do far better. And you'll experience the joy of being not merely a collector of other people's techniques but a creator of your own.

The book is not intended to be read from cover to cover, but to be a resource that you can use again and again for many years to come. However, I recommend that you read and digest the rest of this introduction and the first three chapters to get grounded in the A.L. philosophy. Then you can selectively browse the rest of the book, concentrating on those areas of your greatest interest and need. The initial grounding will help you make more sense out of the rest of the book and allow you to use it more wisely as an aid to your enjoyment and success as a provider of learning experiences for others.

Changing Your Mind

All of us need to reconsider and, in some cases, abandon some of our assumptions about human learning and corporate training. Many of the assumptions in our culture and in us are artifacts of the 19th century and need to be jettisoned if we are to meet the learning challenges of the 21st century.

This book will invite you to abandon any assumptions you might have that are keeping you shackled to the 19th century and to embrace more appropriate assumptions that are bound to make you more successful.

The Many Benefits for You

The wise and continued use of this book will result in a number of positive benefits for you and the people you serve. It will enable you to:

- Ignite your creative imagination
- Get learners totally involved
- Create healthier learning environments
- Speed and enhance learning
- Improve retention and job performance
- Speed the design process
- Build effective learning communities
- Greatly improve technology-driven learning

Implementing A.L. can help your organization save time and money, build a healthier work force, and enjoy a better ROI (return on investment), both financially and operationally.

Oh yes, and one more thing. You will be able to apply many of the techniques in this book to your children at home to improve their learning effectiveness as well.

Some Major Assumptions of A.L.

Here are some of the major assumptions we are making about what people need in order to optimize their learning. You'll find these assumptions woven throughout this book.

A Positive Learning Environment. People learn best in a positive physical, emotional, and social environment, one that is both relaxed and stimulating. A sense of wholeness, safety, interest, and enjoyment is essential for optimizing human learning.

Total Learner Involvement. People learn best when they are totally and actively involved and take full responsibility for their own learning. Learning is not a spectator sport but a participatory one. Knowledge is not something a learner passively absorbs, but something a learner actively creates. Thus

A.L. tends to be more *activity-based* rather than materials-based or presentations-based.

Collaboration Among Learners. People generally learn best in an environment of collaboration. All good learning tends to be social. Whereas traditional learning emphasizes competition between isolated individuals, A.L. emphasizes collaboration between learners in a learning community.

Variety That Appeals to All Learning Styles. People learn best when they have a rich variety of learning options that allows them to use all their senses and exercise their preferred learning style. Rather than thinking of a learning program as a one-dish meal, A.L. thinks of it as a results-driven, learner-centered smorgasbord.

Contextual Learning. People learn best in context. Facts and skills learned in isolation are hard to absorb and quick to evaporate. The best learning comes from doing the work itself in a continual process of "real-world" immersion, feedback, reflection, evaluation, and reimmersion.

Summarizing the Difference

Here's a comparison between some of the characteristics of traditional learning vs. accelerated learning. These are tendencies only and not pure exclusive opposites.

Traditional Learning tends to be:	Accelerated Learning tends to be:
Rigid	Flexible
Somber & serious	Joyful
Single-pathed	Multi-pathed
Means-centered	Ends-centered
Competitive	Collaborative
Behavioristic	Humanistic
Verbal	Multi-sensory
Controlling	Nurturing
Materials-centered	Activity-centered
Mental (cognitive)	Mental/emotional/physical
Time-based	Results-based

The Spirit of the Thing

A.L. is an integrated philosophy of life and of learning. As such, it's a whole new view of things that demechanizes and re-humanizes learning and puts the learner (not the teacher, not the materials, not the presentations) squarely in the center of things.

A.L. is systemic, not cosmetic. You can't do it successfully without having it affect your whole system, your whole self, and your whole organization. People who get the most from A.L. treat it as a way of life. For these people, learners become not vessels to be filled, but fires to be ignited. Learning programs are not seen as propaganda, or indoctrination, or conditioning, or stimulus/response "training", but as vehicles for the nurture of full life and intelligence and spirit in people.

You can ignore many parts of this book and go for those techniques that are most important for you right now. But I wish in my gut that you would not ignore the book's central premise: that in a high-tech culture such as ours, it's essential to keep alive the human element, which is the most important ingredient in learning.

The Joy of Learning

Most books for learning facilitators are devoted to explaining how to use certain prescribed techniques, procedures, methods, and media. It's all very serious stuff. Sad to say, most of those technique-laden books never talk about *the joy of learning*. Yet it's the joy of learning that is often the major determiner of the quality and quantity of learning that can go on.

A.L. practitioners want learners to experience the joy of learning because they know how important it is. This kind of "joy" does not mean hats, horns, and hoopla. It's got nothing to do with mindless bliss and shallow fluff. But this "joy" means interest, connectedness, and the involved and happy creation of meaning and understanding and value *on the part of the learner*. It's the joy of giving birth to something new. And this joy is far more significant for learning than any technique or method or medium you might choose to use.

Recurring Themes

Throughout this book, many of the underlying themes of A.L. recur again and again. This is similar to a symphony or musical composition in which a musical theme is repeated in different contexts to integrate the work. Weaving the basic themes of A.L. throughout this book is a way to tie this book together and provide you with steady and repeated reinforcement as you create your own meaning and value out of the ideas presented.

Lighten Up

Please don't take any of the ideas, statements, or principles in this book as dogmatic absolutes. This book does not attempt to speak the last word about education and training, only a few first words in order to stimulate thought, discussion, and positive action. Use the book as a springboard, if you can, and then go beyond it. It's liberating to know that none of us (and no book) will ever be able to exhaust the creative possibilities for learning and for life.

The Aim of Accelerated Learning

The purpose of A.L. is to awaken learners to their full learning ability, to make learning enjoyable and fulfilling for them again, and to contribute to their full human happiness, intelligence, competence, and success.

Accelerated Learning Is a Result

Accelerated learning is, first and foremost, an end, not a means. Put another way: accelerated learning is the results achieved, not the methods used. It's essential to associate accelerated learning with outcomes and not with particular methods (games, music, color, activities, etc.). Whatever methods work to accelerate and enhance learning are, by this definition, accelerated learning methods. And whatever methods do not produce an accelerated and enhanced learning

Accelerated learning is the results achieved not the methods used.

are not— no matter how clever, or creative, or fun they might be.

So don't get hung up on any specific medium, method, or technique but always keep your eye on the intended result.

A.L: A Philosophy in Tune With the Times

Accelerated learning encompasses a large and ever expanding number of techniques (you'll encounter hundreds of them in this book) but it's far more than that. At heart it's a philosophy of learning and of life that seeks to demechanize and rehumanize the learning process and make it a whole-body, whole-mind, whole-person experience. As such, it seeks to re-form many of the limiting beliefs and practices inherited from the past.

A.L. is part of a larger grass-roots movement taking place today not only in education, but in agriculture, in medicine, in community life, and elsewhere— a movement to recover the real— a movement to realign human life with the natural, the humanistic, the organic— a movement away from the artificial, the mechanistic, and the contrived— and a movement to nurture human intelligence on all levels (rational, emotional, physical, social, intuitive, creative, ecological, spiritual, ethical, etc.) and make learning effective again.

It's Just Natural

Accelerated learning is *natural* learning. It's based on the way people naturally learn. The beautiful thing about A.L. is that we already know all about it instinctively. As children, we practiced it every day of our lives. We learned all the basics not through sitting in a classroom, reading a book, or staring at a computer screen, but through interacting with others and with the world using our whole bodies, our whole minds, our whole selves.

Accelerated Learning is to education and training what organic agriculture is to the factory farm.

Open Bowl Learning: The Child

As children we learn on many levels simultaneously. We are open— as open as a wide-mouthed bowl that receives everything pouring into it from the environment. Learning is fast. Retention is excellent.

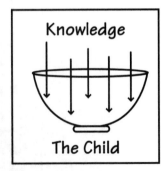

Knowledge

The Child

Pinched Vase Learning: The Adult

But then structured education intervenes. The wide-mouthed bowl of the child is pinched into a narrow-mouthed vase of the adult. Learning now becomes controlled, structured, standardized, mechanized, and exclusively verbal. What enters us now is a linear, one-thing-at-a-time trickle of information doled out to us by the instructional medium, be it a person or machine. Learning invariably deteriorates.

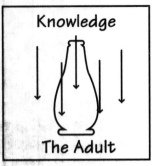

Knowledge

The Adult

Opening Again to Our Full Capacity

Accelerated learning seeks to pry open that narrow mouth of linear learning so that people can become open bowls again, taking in knowledge with all their senses and with their whole selves, learning on many levels simultaneously, learning once more with the power of a child.

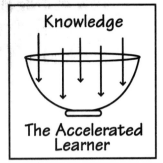

Knowledge

The Accelerated Learner

As it turns out, we adults have far more capacity for learning than has been recognized and utilized by the linear, verbal, cognitive approaches of formalized education. Georgi Lozanov, a seminal researcher in accelerated learning, speaks of "the reserves of the mind." He points out that rational consciousness is just the tip of the iceberg in terms of one's full mental capacity. People learn, he says, on many levels simultaneously, most of which are in addition to the cognitive and verbal processing of rational consciousness.

Whole-Mind, Whole-Body Learning

Research now indicates that people learn through their whole bodies and their whole minds verbally, nonverbally, rationally, emotionally, physically, intuitively— all at the same time.

This would explain why learning simultaneously by immersion is far superior than learning one little thing at a time sequentially off-line and out of context. (This also explains why you could learn more French living with a French family in Paris for three months than you could learn by taking high school French for three years.)

You see now why accelerated learning is concerned about the total context of a learning environment and not merely about the content alone. A.L. seeks to place learners in environments that are positive physically, emotionally, and socially and to give them an experience of learning by immersion that is as close to the real world as possible.

The Revolution in Learning

Nineteenth and early twentieth-century beliefs in the West tended to make learning dreary, slow, and ineffective. And no sophisticated technology or clever "techniques" built upon this old foundation has helped correct the problem. What we need is an entirely new foundation.

The old foundation is based on learners as consumers, on *individual* performance, on compartmentalization (of people and subject matter), on centralized bureaucratic control, on trainers as platform performers, on learning as primarily verbal and cognitive, and on training programs as assembly line processes.

The new foundation is based on learners as creators, on collaboration and *group* performance, on interconnectedness, on learning as a whole mind/body activity, and on learning programs that provide option-rich learning environments for appealing to all learning styles.

Shifting Educational Goals

Nineteenth-Century Learning

The goal of 19th-century education (which still affects the thinking of many people today) was often to train people in narrowly defined external behaviors in order to produce a predictable standardized output. This approach to learning required a dulling of one's complete self. Its quest: to bring behavior into line with routine production and thinking. The task of education and training was to prepare people for a relatively simple, static, and predictable world. The trouble today is that that world no longer exists. And we've been slow to realize it.

Twenty-First-Century Learning

Today, the task of education and training is to prepare people for a world in flux, a world in which everyone needs to exercise their full powers of mind and heart and act out of a sense of mindful creativity, not mindless predictability. Rather than producing "carbon copy" people as in the 19th century, we now need to produce "originals" who can exercise the energy of their full potential and promise. We need to release everyone's unique intelligence and not suppress it in the name of standardization or "company culture." There is no more business as usual. On every level we must all be innovators.

A Return to Wholeness

Of paramount importance in accelerated learning is a sense of wholeness— wholeness of knowledge, of the individual, of the organization, and of life itself. This is in sharp contrast to the compartmentalization of the past. Western science since Aristotle has been concerned about isolating, analyzing, and categorizing the separate elements of existence. This has led to the fragmentation of learning and of life.

Today we need to become whole again. We need to understand that learning is not an isolated cognitive event but something involving a person's whole self (body, mind, and soul) and all of

a person's unique intelligences.

Learners are no longer seen as passive consumers of someone else's information, but as active creators of their own knowledge and skill. Therein lies the revolution, and therein lies the unique contribution of the ideas and methods you'll discover in this book.

Organizational Payoffs

Accelerated Learning is paying off handsomely for many organizations. Here are just a few examples.

A major US semiconductor manufacturer improved by 507% the measurable learning in a course on safety and hazardous chemicals. The company did it by creating a learning smorgasbord in which learners could choose their own path through the curriculum from an array of options (print media, audio, video). And collaboration among learners was encouraged throughout.

Travelers Insurance did side-by-side pilots, comparing conventional training methods with accelerated learning ones for teaching a new computerized system to claim adjusters. In the conventional class, 12% of the learners received test scores of 85 and above. In the A.L. group, 67% tested at 85 and above (an improvement of over 400%). And they did it in 20% less time. The secret? Stress reduction, collaboration among learners, and the use of imagery mnemonics.

Florida Community College used A.L. methods to improve computer learning by a factor of four by putting two people to a computer and making them responsible for one another's learning.

Bell Atlantic cut training time in half and improved measurable job performance when they converted their initial training of customer service reps to an A.L. format. The new training emphasized an emotionally stimulating environment, variety in training methods, total learner involvement, and collaboration among learners.

> It works. Using accelerated learning techniques on two of our major courses, we have been able to cut training time virtually in half while significantly improving learning and job performance.
>
> —Mary Jane Gill
> Training Manager
> Bell Atlantic

US West, in preparing new hires to be customer service reps for their cellular phone business, found conventional methods (lecture, reading, etc.) to be ineffective. So they had learners act out cellular systems, individual learners playing the roles of cellular phones, cell sites (transmission towers), and land-line equipment (for non-cellular phones), and establishing various connections with a rope. Instructors Shirley Walker and Mike Patricks found this to be overwhelmingly superior to conventional classroom methods in speeding and optimizing everyone's learning.

AGFA designers Lynn Brown and Jerry DelVecchio upgraded an existing teambuilding course with an A.L. version that they designed in just one hour. They cut course time from 8 1/2 hours to 6, improving the learning. The new program, they say, is all activity based and gets the learners totally involved, which accounts for its great success.

Personal Payoffs

The personal payoffs that A.L. practitioners are enjoying are just as exciting as they experience unprecedented success with the methods. Many claim that A.L. has changed their lives. They report finding new creative energy for their work, as they are able to design faster, improve learning and job performance, bring more creativity and joy to the workplace, and have a whale of a good time doing it. For example:

Terri Schoedel of GE Capital wrote us these words: "Accelerated Learning is revolutionary. It has improved learner and trainer productivity in our organization immeasurably. The learners are stimulated, liberated, and ultimately more spirited. Accelerated Learning techniques are triumphant to say the least."

Daphne Fitzgerald, President of Zurich Canada's Group Insurance Division is equally enthusiastic: "There's no doubt in my mind that the accelerated learning approach is the ideal strategy for our business. We have achieved immediate and measurable results with the programs we have developed."

Charlie King of Southern Nuclear says: "Since we started using A.L., our instructors have never been as concerned about making training more interesting, creative, and fun. How do students like it? We've never had better feedback."

Joan Shuckenbrock, when training manager for Continental Airlines, wrote us these words after her staff was trained in accelerated learning: "It's a joy to come to work again because everyone is being so creative."

Benjamin Harris of People's Energy Co. says: " A.L. has proven to be a recharger for body, soul, and mind for someone who thought he knew what experiential education was all about."

And There's More

The following page contains a summary of some of the results companies are experiencing. And you'll find many other examples of A.L. successes scattered throughout this book.

Achievements of A.L. Practitioners

Here's a small sampling of what some organizations have experienced with A.L.

Company	Application	Results
American Airlines	Reservationists Training	Reduced training time for a lesson by 50%. Improved the retention significantly.
Bell Atlantic	Customer Service Rep	Cut training time in half while improving measurable performance.
Chevron	Fire Extinguisher Training	Reduced training time by 50% while achieving same or better learning.
Consolidated Edison	Cable Splicing Course	Passing rate increased from 30% to 100% in same time.
Commonwealth Edison	Time Keeper Training	Cut class time in half while greatly improving test scores, long-term retention and student evaluations.
Florida Community College	Lotus 1-2-3 Course	Students learned 75% faster while enjoying the training much more.
Fortune 100 Midwest Manufacturer	Inventory Management Course	Reduced training time by 60% while improving learning.
Kodak	Electronics Course	Cut training time by a third and improved long-term retention by 25%.
Major US Semiconductor Manufacturer	Hazcom and Safety Training	Improved measurable learning by 507% in the same time frame.
Bell Atlantic	Telephone Skills Training	Cut training time by 50% and doubled the learning.
Travelers Insurance	Medical Claim Benefits Training	Cut training time by 20% improving test scores by 480%.
Major Retail Chain	Coaching Skills for Managers	Reduced training time by 75% while achieving better results.

Obviously, there is something going on here.

PART 1

The Learning Revolution

CHAPTER 1

A Brief History
of the A.L. Movement

Accelerated Learning:
A Time-Honored Practice

Since accelerated learning (A.L.) is *natural* learning, its roots go far back into antiquity. (It has been practiced by every child ever born.) But in terms of a modern movement to revolutionize learning within *structured* education and training in Western culture, it sprung from a number of influences during the last half of the 20th Century.

The Lozanov Approach

In the 1970s, Lynn Schroeder and Sheila Ostrander published a book called *Superlearning* that reported on the work of Bulgarian psychiatrist Georgi Lozanov. It got the attention of many educators and teachers searching for more effective approaches to learning.

Lozanov found that by relaxing psychiatric patients with Baroque music and giving them positive suggestions about their healing, many made substantial progress. He had found a way, he felt, to tap into something in the psyche deeper than rational consciousness. (He called this "the hidden reserves of the mind.")

He felt that these methods could be applied to education as well. Under sponsorship of the Bulgarian government he began doing research into the effects of music and positive suggestion on learning using foreign language as the subject matter. He found that the combination of music, suggestions, and childlike play allowed learners to learn significantly faster and more effectively. Word of his discovery ignited the imaginations of

language teachers and nonstandard educators everywhere.

In the 1970's, Don Schuster, of Iowa State University, and educators Ray Bordon and Charles Gritton, began applying these methods to high school and university teaching with positive results. In 1975 they and others established SALT (The Society for Accelerative Learning and Teaching) and began sponsoring international conferences that attracted college professors, public school educators, and corporate trainers from around the world. SALT is now in its 25th year. It has renamed itself IAL (The International Alliance for Learning) and still sponsors annual conferences in the United States for an international audience.

England has a similar group called S.E.A.L. (Society for Effective Affective Learning), and practitions in Germany have formed D.S.G.L. (The German Society for Suggestopedic Teaching and Learning).

Other Influences on the Growth of A.L.

Many other factors have contributed to a steady and sustained growth in A.L. philosophies, methods, and applications. Here are just a few of them.

1. Modern cognitive science, particularly research into the brain and learning, has thrown into question many of our old assumptions about learning. Gone is the notion that learning is simply a verbal, "cognitive," head thing. Current research indicates that the best learning involves the emotions, the whole body, all the senses, and the full breadth and depth of the personality (what Lozanov would call "the hidden reserves of the mind").

2. Learning styles research has indicated that different people learn in different ways and that one size does not fit all. This has seriously challenged our idea of formal education and training as a cookie-cutter, assembly line process.

3. The collapse of the Newtonian world view (that nature works like a machine, automatically obedient to independent, linear, step-by-step processes) and the rise of

quantum physics has given us a new appreciation for the interconnectedness of all things and for the nonlinear, non-mechanistic, creative, and "alive" nature of reality.

4. The gradual (yet incomplete) evolution from a male dominant culture to one that balances male and female sensibilities is allowing for more of a gentle, collaborative, and nurturing approach to learning.

5. The decline of Behaviorism as the dominant psychology in learning has led to the rise of more humanistic and holistic beliefs and practices.

6. Several parallel movements in the 20th century have kept alive alternate educational approaches: The Progressive School Movement starting in the 1920s, the Confluent Education Movement starting in the the 40s, the Humanistic Education Movement starting in the 50s, and the Free School Movement of the 60s. Also of some influence have been the Montessori Schools of Maria Montessori, the Waldorf Schools of Rudolph Steiner, and the Summerhill School movement in England championed by Alexander Sutherland Neill.

7. The constantly changing nature of the workplace and of culture itself has rendered many of our methods of education and training slow and obsolete and has opened the door to alternative approaches.

The Growth of A.L. in Corporations

In 1986, Mary Jane Gill, a training director at Bell Atlantic, attended a workshop on A.L. in Lake Geneva, Wisconsin, sponsored by the *Center for Accelerated Learning*.

She returned home and arranged for one of Bell Atlantic's old, obsolete courses for customer service rep training to be re-written in an A.L. format. The results were dramatic. Training time was cut in half while learning and job performance improved measurably.

Mary Jane and I coauthored an article on this success titled

Accelerated Learning Takes Off at Bell Atlantic that appeared in the *Journal of the American Society for Training and Development* in January of 1989.

The word was out. All the major U.S. phone companies then joined in and began applying A.L. techniques to their customer service rep training with very positive results. Other organizations followed suit and A.L., still far from the mainstream, became an alternative that was proving itself over and over as a way to speed and enhance learning for corporate training departments.

An Expanding Movement

As with any new departure from the norm, A.L. has sometimes been misidentified as merely games and clever techniques (without a deep understanding of, and commitment to, its underlying principles) and thus has suffered some false starts. And once in a while rogues and semi-rouges have rushed in who have been more interested in making money than making changes and have missed the point completely. And then there has been the ever present inertia of traditional educational approaches that has tended to erode fresh new starts over time in order to return to the comfortable but deadly norm.

But despite all this, A.L. has survived and thrived in the minds and hearts of many teachers and trainers who resonate with its humanistic, holistic, and positive spiritual center. And they're making a difference.

As of this writing, hundreds of organizations have had their staffs educated in accelerated learning philosophies and methods. Though there is still a long way to go, A.L. is becoming increasingly accepted as a new standard for teaching and learning in many corporations and, happily, even in a number of forward-looking community colleges and schools.

Because of the substantial value it is bringing to people and to organizations, the number of A.L. practitioners in the U.S., Canada, and all over the world is growing daily.

Making History

To write a full history of A.L. and to mention all the people who have played and are playing seminal roles in its growth in corporations and schools would fill this book. We will spare you the details so that you can get on with the business of joining them and making your own history as a facilitator of accelerated learning methods where you live and work.

CHAPTER 2

The Guiding Principles
of Accelerated Learning

To get the most out of using accelerated learning, it's essential to get a firm grasp on its underlying principles. A.L. will fail for those who abstract its methods from its ideological underpinnings, reducing A.L. to clever gimmicks and creative "techniques" while ignoring the principles on which those techniques are based.

A.L. training programs that are the most successful operate out of the following foundation principles:

1. **Learning Involves the Whole Mind and Body.** Learning is not at all merely "head" learning (conscious, rational, "left-brained," and verbal) but involves the whole body/mind with its all its emotions, senses, and receptors.

2. **Learning Is Creation, Not Consumption.** Knowledge is not something a learner absorbs, but something a learner creates. Learning happens when a learner integrates new knowledge and skill into his or her existing structure of self. Learning is literally a matter of *creating* new meanings, new neural networks, and new patterns of electro/chemical interactions within one's total brain/body system.

3. **Collaboration Aids Learning.** All good learning has a social base. We often learn more by interacting with peers than we learn by any other means. Competition between learners slows learning. Cooperation among learners speeds it. A genuine learning community is always better for learning than a collection of isolated individuals.

4. **Learning Takes Place on Many Levels Simultaneously.** Learning is not a matter of absorbing one little thing at a time in linear fashion, but absorbing many things at once. Good

learning engages people on many levels simultaneously (conscious and paraconscious, mental and physical) and uses all the receptors and senses and paths it can into a person's total brain/body system. The brain, after all, is not a sequential, but a parallel processor and thrives when it is challenged to do many things at once.

5. **Learning Comes From Doing the Work Itself (With Feedback).** People learn best in context. Things learned in isolation are hard to remember and quick to evaporate. We learn how to swim by swimming, how to manage by managing, how to sing by singing, how to sell by selling, and how to care for customers by caring for customers. The real and the concrete are far better teachers than the hypothetical and the abstract— provided there is time for total immersion, feedback, reflection, and reimmersion.

6. **Positive Emotions Greatly Improve Learning.** Feelings determine both the quality and quantity of one's learning. Negative feelings inhibit learning. Positive feelings accelerate it. Learning that is stressful, painful, and dreary can't hold a candle to learning that is joyful, relaxed, and engaging.

7. **The Image Brain Absorbs Information Instantly and Automatically.** The human nervous system is more of an image processor than a word processor. Concrete images are much easier to grasp and retain than are verbal abstractions. Translating verbal abstractions into concrete images of all kinds will make those verbal abstractions faster to learn and easier to remember.

CHAPTER 3

Curing the West's Educational Diseases

Most of us adults are learning disabled and we don't even know it. What has disabled us (and continues to do so) are learning beliefs and practices inherited from the past and now integrated into our culture.

These disabling beliefs and practices, representing centuries old trends in the West, came to final institutionalized form in the 19th century with the establishment of the compulsory education system in the United States. Now they're embedded in both public education and corporate training like entrenched diseases that are hard to shake.

What makes these 19th-century assumptions about learning so powerful and deadly is that they are hidden— taken for granted as the way things have been, are, and always will be. Few people question these assumptions. Fewer yet have taken steps to overcome them. Obviously we need a revolution in our whole approach to learning so we can rid ourselves of the culturally imposed beliefs and practices that have made learning so dismal, unnatural, difficult, and ineffective for so many people.

One way to rid ourselves of these debilitating beliefs and practices is to understand where they came from and how they got planted in us in the first place. Once we've done that, we're no longer obliged to blindly perpetuate them. Rather we are free to creatively construct new and more effective approaches to learning. If this is something you want to do, read on.

The West's Educational Diseases

What follows is a look at some of the major 19th-century "diseases" that have infected our educational beliefs and practices in the West, and some suggestions for cure. Of course, all of these diseases are interrelated and have fed each other, but for the purpose of this analysis we can look at them one at a time.

The Diseases:

1. Puritanism
2. Individualism
3. The Factory Model
4. Western Scientific Thought
5. Mind/Body Separation
6. Male Dominance
7. The Printing Press

Disease #1: Puritanism

In 19th-century America, the first compulsory education system (known as the Common School Movement) took shape in New England and became the model for institutionalized education in the rest of the country. New England, of course, was colonized by the Puritans, and their philosophies exerted a profound influence on all the institutions of the New England culture. The assumptions of Puritanism, then, quite naturally became embedded in the very foundation of American education.

Learning, for the Puritans, was indoctrination— often a dreary, joyless, and rote affair. John Robinson, a Pilgrim teacher and leader, summed up the Puritan attitude toward education in his essay, *Children and Their Education* as quoted by A.M. Earle in his 1899 book *Child Life in Colonial Days*.

> Surely there is in all children a stubbornness and
> stoutness of minde arising from natural pride
> which must in the first place be broken and beaten
> down so that the foundation of their education
> being layd in humilitie and tractableness, other
> virtues may in their time be build thereon.

Then he went on to compare educating a child to training a horse to take the bit in its mouth and a rider on its back. As Ichabod Crane, the school master in Washington Irving's *The Legend of Sleepy Hollow* summed it up: "Spare the rod and spoil the child."

Discipline was central to the early system. So much so that some citizens felt that there was little time left for actual learning. But their concerns were overruled by the strong Puritan influence. Pain and corporal punishment were felt to be essential components of child education. The old song *School Days* written in 1906 says it all:

> School days, school days,
> Dear old Golden Rule days!
> Reading and writing an 'rithmetic
> Taught to the tune of a hickory stick!

There you have it. The hickory stick. The marriage of pain and learning. Banished is the sense of joy and freedom in learning. Replacing it is the notion of rigor, starkness, stress, incarceration, control from above, and a conscious avoidance of pleasure. (As Mark Twain once said, "Puritanism is characterized by the haunting fear that someone somewhere might be happy.") And so the notion of pain and the notion of learning got fused in the American educational system. It still is for many people...unconsciously.

In academia the marriage of pain and learning is all too evident. Of course this varies greatly from school to school and from teacher to teacher, but often "no pain no gain" is the hidden belief. Joyful, stressless learning is suspect. Exuberance, passion, and wild creativity must be suppressed and tamed. Rigor and cold, analytical logic are deemed to be the only true paths to knowledge. A certain degree of mental suffering is felt to be inevitable in the quest for knowledge.

The Puritan influence is deeply embedded in many corporations as well. For instance, what do you suppose is the automatic knee-jerk reaction of the average corporate executive who hears laughter and frivolity coming from a training room? Most likely it's something like, "Why don't these people get down to

It sounds like something Yogi Berra might say, but the trouble with the Pilgrims was that they were so Puritanical. And education and training in the U.S. has been suffering from this ever since.

business and start learning?" And so it is that in many corporate cultures today, too much joy and exuberance are seen as antithetical to learning. So now, instead of *corporal* punishment, we've got *corporate* punishment, requiring people to learn in dreary, sterile environments through boring lectures, interminable PowerPoint presentations, deadly manuals, mind-numbing computer programs, and a remarkable absence of joy. Ichabod Crane is still very much with us.

Edward T. Hall in his spirited 1976 book *Beyond Culture* put his finger on it when he said:

> "Somehow in the United States we have managed to transform one of the most rewarding of all human activities (i.e., learning) into a painful, boring, dull, fragmenting, mind-shrinking, soul-shriveling experience."

 The Cure

The best antidote to Puritanism, according to accelerated learning theory, is to restore the joy to learning. Both children and adults do best in learning environments characterized by personal interest and happiness, and not in environments characterized by intimidation, boredom, stress, irrelevance, or pain. The "joy" that is an essential ingredient of accelerated learning has nothing to do with mindless bliss or shallow, hats-and-horns hoopla, but is a deep and quiet peace and a sense of connectedness, wholeness, and involvement. Accelerated learning practitioners are always searching for ways to make learning joyful again, in the deepest meaning of that word, because they know that a sense of joy is at the heart of all exceptional learning.

When your soul is happy, your learning is snappy.

We have a great deal to learn from small children about this. They are the greatest accelerated learners in the world because they learn with such joy. Therefore, if you have a dry, boring, and mind-numbing subject to teach, ask yourself, "How would I teach this to children? How can I make learning this a joyful experience?" Asking and answering these questions again and again over time will cure any addiction you and your organization might have to educational Puritanism. And learning will improve dramatically. Enhanced learning stems from a sense of joy for children and adults alike.

Disease #2: Individualism

American education has been a reflection of the culture in which it was born. And that culture was steeped in individualism— individual salvation, the lone pioneer, and the individual entrepreneur struggling alone and winning against all odds. Most societies throughout history believed differently. They centered their life in the family, the tribe, the group. Not so in America. "Each man for himself" became the unwritten law of the land.

Driven by this bias toward excessive individualism, universities developed with almost no sense of the social nature of learning. Rather, education emphasized individual achievement. Grading was strictly individualistic and sometimes based on a curve— so many A's, so many B's. Learners thus competed with each other for grades and high honors. It was thought to be the purpose of higher education to produce strong, self-reliant individuals who could work independently and in isolation (as the early settlers often had to do). And competition among these isolated learners was thought to be a goad toward greater individual achievement. The unspoken rule was: "Learn from your teacher and compete with your peers."

Thus education and training often became a matter of solitary confinement, and there was very little emphasis on learning in groups. The behavioristic teaching machines that were introduced into schools and corporations after the 2nd World War were placed, of course, in individual carrels. Likewise, CAI (computer-aided instruction) that followed the flop of these teaching machines kept the same "learning in isolation" philosophy. More recent multimedia learning systems have done no better, often retaining the same addiction to the individualistic learning approach. And now it's on to the Web.

Our sense of
individualism—
that each of us is alone
and separate—
is a culturally implanted
hallucination.
     –Alan Watts

Here we go again.

This addiction to excessive individualism and competition in education and training has cost us dearly. Isolation has often raised stress levels and reduced the speed, quality, and durability of learning. And the competitive approach has often made learners reluctant to ask questions and seek help from one another, choking off the free flow of information, knowledge, intelligence, and learning.

 **The Cure**

All good learning is social. At least for the overwhelming majority of people. When people help each other learn (whether children or adults), learning improves significantly. Research at the University of Minnesota, for instance, has indicated that, when learning from computers, if you put two people together on one machine and structure it so that they dialog with each other and take responsibility for each other, both the quality and the quantity of learning goes up for both of them.

A study at Stanford University (H.M. Levine, "Cost and Cost-Effectiveness of Computer-Assisted Instruction) found that peer tutoring was four times more effective for improving math and reading achievement than either reduced class size or lengthened instruction time, and significantly more effective than individual computer-based instruction.

In the training world, I have seen miracles occur when a class changed from a collection of isolated individuals to a learning community. I have seen learning speed and retention increase by more than 300% (in a computer class at Florida Community College), failure rates drop from 40% to 2% (in a customer service rep training program at Bell Atlantic), test scores improve by more than 400% (in a claims processing course at Travelers Insurance). The reason? Most people learn better in community than they do in isolation. When everyone in a learning group is a teacher and a learner simultaneously, the stress level goes way down and the learning shoots way up.

If you do nothing else to improve learning, get people to work together in partnerships, small teams, or as a whole group. It will have an immediate and profound effect on the learning. This is because, despite how our educational institutions have conditioned us, the best kind of learning has a strong social base.

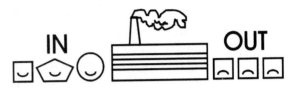

Disease #3: The Factory Model

Formalized American education was defined in New England during the full flower of the Industrial Revolution. The men who put together America's "common schools" in New England were greatly influenced by the factory model which surrounded them on all sides. The early schools were, in fact, the conscious and "scientific" application of mass production techniques to public education.

And so, the assembly line school was born— with everything sequenced, controlled, compartmentalized, and standardized by the central office. Children were separated by age. Curriculum was prescribed for each stage of the production process. Everyone adhered to the strict timings of the production schedule. (Eight years of this and four years of that— ka-chunk, ka-chunk, ka-chunk.) Teachers became production line supervisors. Production came to be run by the numbers. And a huge bureaucracy arose to control, measure, and manage this whole gigantic enterprise.

Some schools became no more than detention homes for warehousing the young; penal institutions where children were forced to "do time" for a prescribed number of years. (The term, "We're out of school!" is still synonymous with "We're out of prison!") But today the prisoners are escaping from the factory schools in unprecedented numbers, particularly in the big cities. As of this writing, Boston's school drop-out rate is about 45%. New York City's is close to 70%. Obviously the factory model of school is no longer working. And it's ironic. We abandon old factories and production processes for new

> Our schools are, in a sense, factories in which the raw products (children) are to be shaped and fashioned into products to meet the various demands of life.
> –from a 1916 book on school administration by E.P. Cubberly

ones when their technology becomes obsolete, but we won't do the same with the schools. It seems we are too addicted to the factory model of education to have any real clue as to what to do to truly reform education in our time.

The factory schools have had a profound effect on corporate training as well. The one-path, standardized, cookie-cutter, time-based, and classroom-confined (and computer-confined) approach to learning became the norm. Corporate training tended to become overly formalized, compartmentalized, disconnected, and artificial. And learners often sensed the great disparity between many standardized corporate training programs and "the real world."

Assembly line learning forced a one-size-fits-all linearity on everyone and often resulted in hobbled learning, poor transference, and a huge waste of time and money. Many corporations now hope that a new assembly line— the computer and the web— will solve all their training problems. It won't. All we're doing is automating the assembly line, putting stale wine in new bottles and calling it progress. We're still hoping for one standardized solution. Our addiction to one-size-fits-all assembly line learning still controls us.

 **The Cure**

According to accelerated learning theory, the one-dish meal of education and training needs to be replaced with a smorgasbord if we are to optimize learning for everyone. There is not one best way. There are many. There is not one single path to successful learning. There are many. Our devotion to either/or thinking must give place to both/and thinking if we are to fulfill the promise of accelerated learning.

By concentrating on ends, not means, we'll lose our addiction to the one-size-fits-all approach of assembly line learning and we'll be able to achieve better results. Computers? Sure. Classrooms? Sure. Mentoring programs? Sure. The Web? Sure. Team-based learning? Certainly. Self-paced learning? You bet'cha. Embedded learning? Absolutely. You can use whatever gets the job done for different people and different solutions. The same subject matter can be cast into many different forms to appeal to the full range of personality types and learning styles. People can be made responsible for their own learning as they choose their own path to competence from an array of options. Learning is enhanced when it is a smorgasbord rather than a one-dish meal.

Disease #4: Western Scientific Thinking

The scientific worldview that developed from the 16th century on formed the modern world.

Two pivotal beliefs (owing to the work of Rene Descartes, Isaac Newton, and others) helped shape this worldview:

1. There are two separate realms, the outer world of physical nature, and the inner world of nonphysical mind. (This is often referred to as the body-mind split.)

2. Each separate component in the outer world of nature (the human body included) is like a well-ordered machine that operates according to predetermined mechanical laws that we can learn how to understand and manipulate. The inner world of mind and spirit is, by comparison, of much less concern and consequence.

These beliefs spawned the industrial and technological revolution in the West that changed the course of history, brought unprecedented wealth to civilization, and raised the standard of living in many positive ways for hundreds of millions of people.

But this mechanistic worldview also brought with it some unwanted baggage: it led to the despiritualization of the world, the exploitation of nature, excessive competitive individualism, the dehumanization of work life, and human alienation on many levels.

When applied to social thinking, the mechanistic worldview became the foundation for the psychology of behaviorism, a

> Western science came to believe that each separate component of nature was like a soulless clockwork mechanism, operating independently according to its own separate predetermined laws. What a cuckoo idea!

major influence on training for the bulk of the 20th century. Behaviorism's concern was with finding ways to manipulate one's *external* behavior while ignoring the relevancy of one's inner world. It sought to "engineer" people's external performance as if human beings were machines to be manipulated. (Serious behaviorists and many practitioners of Neuro-Linguistic Programming still believe this, from what I can tell.)

Too, the mechanistic worldview believed nature to be made up of separate disconnected parts, each operating according to its own prescribed laws. This led to the fragmentation of knowledge and learning. Learning was divided into separate subjects, each one taught in isolation. Subjects were often taught "off-line" in strict linear fashion, disconnected from their simultaneous and systemic interrelationships with other factors in the real worlds.

Non-contextual, piecemeal and mechanical teaching approaches allowed people to be programmed to make quick robotic responses within a narrow framework, but often left them spiritually weak, passionless, emotionally isolated, and without the ability to think outside the box and create new possibilities for themselves and their organizations.

If you're interested in exploring the effects of the mechanistic worldview further, here are a few books that I can recommend: *The Corrupted Sciences,* A. Arnold, Harper Collins, 1992; *The Quantum Society,* Danah Zohar, William Morrow, 1994; *Descartes' Error,* Antonio Damasio, Putnam, 1994; and *The Resurgence of the Real,* Charlene Spretnak, Routledge, 1999.

 **The Cure**

We can help heal the devastating effect of the mechanistic worldview on learning by having people learn holistically and in context. Since experience is the greatest teacher, it's best that people not merely learn about a subject off-line, but (as much as possible) experience it firsthand in its real-world setting. This is messier, has more ambiguity, and may not be as easy to control, but the cycle of real-world trial, feedback, and retrial is many times more effective than off-line learning. You don't learn best by listening to a lecture or staring at a computer screen. You learn best by experience, by doing the work itself.

Whereas traditional instructional design emphasizes learning one thing at a time in nice, neat, logical sequence, accelerated learning emphasizes learning many things simultaneously in a real-world environment. Learning is best when it is holistic, not piecemeal, when it is broadly humanistic, not narrowly behavioristic.

Today, the emphasis in education and training should not be to teach people how to store information or respond mechanically to stimuli as much as it should be to teach people how to think, how to navigate information, and how to create meaning and value out of experience.

Paulo Friere in his book *Pedagogy of the Oppressed* says that education should pose problems for people to solve, rather than give pat answers for people to memorize. A problem-posing approach to a subject will generally yield far better results in the long run than an answer-giving approach. The linear learning of Western science is no match for contextual learning that is non-linear, experiential, multi-layered, and whole-brained.

Disease #5: Mind/Body Separation

Western scientific thinking has not only disconnected individuals from nature and from a holistic experience of the world, it has likewise disconnected individuals within themselves. Just as everything in nature was thought of as separate and distinct, so was the mind and the body. The rational mind, then, became the focus of education, and the body was thought of as being totally irrelevant to the learning process. Learning became rational, verbal, abstract, and sedentary. Physical movement was thought not only to be unnecessary, but to be a distraction, and, in many cases, to be a sign of low intelligence or of an inherent learning disability.

School Entrance
Requirement

The bias against the body as a vehicle of learning is profound and widespread in Western culture. "Sit still, don't wiggle, and learn!" is the rule. Edward T. Hall pointed to this bias back in 1976 in an observation about American schooling that could just as well have been written today:

> "The way children are treated in schools is sheer madness. Those who can't sit still are stuck with the hyperactive label and treated as anomalies and frequently drugged."

Corporations too have inherited this bias against the body. Most training is done sitting down— sometimes for hours at a time. Once in a while there may be a stretch break or a formalized "energizer," but these are not generally connected with the learning itself. Learning is still thought of as something done by the disembodied intellect alone and there is little concern about keeping people's whole bodies involved in the learning process, whether in the classroom or on the Web.

 **The Cure**

Modern research has shown us how very inaccurate the notion of a body/mind split is. The mind and the body are not two separate entities, as we have supposed, but one inseparable and integrated whole. In fact, the mind (as research has demonstrated again and again) is not confined to the brain, but is distributed throughout the body. And the body affects the brain in so many ways. Not only does body movement improve brain circulation, but it produces chemicals essential for neural network construction in the brain. As Candice Pert has shown in her book *The Molecules of Emotion*, even molecules think, have memories, and have emotional lives of their own as they move throughout the body/mind and interact with it.

In a very real sense, the mind is the body and the body is the mind.

Carla Hannaford in her book *Smart Moves: Why Learning Is Not All In Your Head* reviews much of the evidence of the inseparable connection between the mind and the body. She points out that the frontal lobe of the brain, prominent in thinking and problem solving, also contains the Primary Motor Area which controls muscles all over the body. Thinking and movement are related in the brain.

Imagine what this means. Whenever we force children to sit quietly and solve problems or force adults to sit quietly and do strategic planning, we are inhibiting their full thinking and learning ability. So let's change that. Let's create learning experiences for people that get the body and the mind to work together actively again.

This book is filled with real-world examples of the great successes that A.L. practitioners are having in creating learning programs that reunite the body and the mind. And this book will give you all sorts of ideas of what you can do to foster a healthier mind/body connection in your programs. It's true for many people much of the time that "If your body don't move, your brain don't groove." Keep chanting that to yourself. It will help you overcome the dreaded disease of mind/body separation.

Disease #6: Male Dominance

Western culture is paternalistic— as if you hadn't noticed. It has tended for centuries to emphasize "male" sensibilities over "female" ones. And this over-masculinization has had a profound effect on all of our educational institutions in the West.

As an example, *the people who put together the first compulsory educational system in the United States in 19th-century Massachusetts were all men.* Women had absolutely no input into it. The system was, from the beginning, a guy's thing, reflecting male perceptions and ways of dealing with reality. Not only the administrators, but all teachers in the new compulsory education system were men. "School Masters" they were called. Women did not become teachers until later when men discovered that they would work for less money. Once you realize that the structure of public education in the West was an exclusively male invention, everything else begins to fall into place and make sense.

Reflecting the paternalistic and sexist character of Western culture, Aristotle believed, and Thomas Aquinas agreed, that women were defective men.

To avoid an overly simplistic gender dichotomy here, we can use the hormones **testosterone** and **estrogen as** loose metaphors. These hormones reside in men and women alike in various mixtures and degrees, there being generally more testosterone in men and more estrogen in women. Here's the sorts of behaviors these hormones tend to produce (according to research and what we can tell from common observation). These are tendencies only, and are not mutually exclusive, and reside in men and women alike to various degrees.

Testosterone Attributes	Estrogen Attributes
Exclusiveness	Inclusiveness
Competition	Collaboration
Emphasis on hierarchy	Emphasis on community
Dominance behaviors	Nurturing behaviors
Sequential thinking	Simultaneous thinking
Logic	Intuition
One right way	Many right ways
Rigid & dogmatic	Flexible & conditional

Corporate training too has tended to be biased toward the male in how it structures itself and in what it supports. One obvious evidence of this is the "HRD Hall of Fame" promoted by Lakewood Publications, publisher of *Training Magazine* and a division of Bill Communications (controlled mainly by guys). For the past 15 years, it has been the men, not the women, that have gotten the accolades. Look at the list of Hall of Fame inductees printed below.

Don't get me wrong. I have no quibble with any of the men on this list. They deserve all the honors they have been given. These men have made tremendous contributions to the field of training. They are exemplary human beings. But despite all that, **where in all of God's green earth are the women?** Observe:

HRD Hall of Fame

Year	Inductee	Gender	Year	Inductee	Gender
1985	Dugan Laird	M	1988	Joe Harless	M
	Bob Mager	M	1990	Martin Broadwell	M
	Gordon Lippitt	M	1991	Ben Tregoe	M
	Thomas Gilbert	M	1992	Ken Blanchard	M
	Malcolm Knowles	M	1993	Pat McLagan	F
1986	George Odiorne	M	1994	Jack Zenger	M
	Geary Rummler	M	1995	Ned Herrmann	M
1987	Len Nadler	M	1996	Peter Block	M
	Robert Blake	M	1998	Gloria Geary	F
	Jane Mouton	F	1999	Scott Parry	M
1988	Warren Bennis	M			

18 men = 85.7% • 3 women = 14.3%
Diagnosis: Hormone imbalance

 **The Cure**

If you look at the failures of education and training today, you have to conclude that, combined with all the other ailments above, there is just too much testosterone in the system. We need a feminine touch in education and training. It's not a matter of abandoning the masculine but achieving **balance**— balance between the male and the female, balance between the right brain and the left, balance between control and nurture, balance between yin and yang.

The interest in Accelerated Learning has paralleled the rise of the feminine influence in Western culture. And as more corporate learning professions and college teachers bring more of the feminine attributes into learning, the more our approaches to learning will achieve a healthy balance— and the better will be the results. Accelerated Learning does not say "Eliminate the masculine!" but "Bring the feminine up to a parity with the masculine!" Good learning and healthy life is a mix between the two. It's never a matter of either/or, but always a matter of both/and. Balance.

Though we are making progress, we still have a ways to go to restore a balance between testosterone and estrogen in our systems of learning and in our culture at large. Academic institutions still tend to be biased toward "maleness." Candice Pert, in her book *The Molecules of Emotion,* recounts some of the obstacles and put-offs she experienced as a researcher in the academic halls of the male scientific establishment.

Disease #7: The Printing Press

We may not realize it now since books are so widespread, but the printing press, invented by Johannes Gutenberg in the 1440s, has had a profound and abiding effect on education and training in the West. It has:

1. Emphasized words over images.

2. Made learning a linear, one-thing-at-a-time process.

3. Emphasized abstract concepts over concrete experience in learning.

4. Elevated the "masculine" left brain over the "feminine" right brain.

5. Supported individualism over collaboration in learning.

The Elevation of Verbal Intelligence

Before the invention of the printing press when the majority of the population was illiterate, learning was driven by concrete experience, by oral tradition, by face-to-face contact, by group life, by pictures and images and symbols, and by immersion into a total context. Learning was a holographic, gestalt, concrete affair. It had to be.

Gutenberg's invention changed all that. Books became widespread. Verbal abstractions stole the show from concrete experience. People no longer had to immerse themselves in real-world contexts or hang out with others in order to learn. They could learn in isolation all by themselves by reading books.

Words in books, then, became the standard tool for acquiring knowledge. The fact that words must be processed sequentially added to the left-brain turn of Western mind. As the book became the major vehicle for education, learning came to emphasize a mechanical, linear, one-thing-at-a-time process. And so today, the more books you read and the more verbal symbols you can manipulate, the more "educated" you are considered to be in our Gutenberg-centered learning culture. And you'll never get the highest of earned academic degrees until you write your own book (called a dissertation).

Books **are** good tools for learning. But by themselves, without the balance of whole-brain experience, they can be deficient in creating genuine knowledge and understanding. True learning is a matter of both/and— both books and experience, both words and images, both left brain and right, both sequential and simultaneous processing, both abstract reflection and concrete experience

But thanks to the printing press, education and training today tend to be almost exclusively left-brained and word-based. When we think of designing training materials, what comes to mind are WORDS: words in reference materials, words in student workbooks, words on overheads, words in PowerPoint presentations, words on computer screens— words, words, words. Training designers become mainly word crafters, forgetting that they need to be image crafters and experience crafters as well.

Educational Emphasis

Before Gutenberg	After Gutenberg
concrete experience	abstract concepts
images	words
whole-brain learning	left-brain learning
holographic processing	linear processing
learning by doing	learning by reading
learning in context	learning off line
learning with others	learning by yourself

The Cure

Both books and concrete experience contribute to our learning. There are times when everything in both lists (on previous page) can be used to help us learn. But it's still true that:

> If you seek information, read words.
> If you seek understanding, have experiences.

> To make learning more effective it needs to be experience-based more than exclusively word-based, whether in the classroom or on the Web.

> Yet when designing learning programs, we often put most of our time, money, and energy into creating presentations and learning materials. But people learn more from experiences (with feedback) than they will ever learn from presentations and materials, no matter how polished they might be.

Accelerated learning, therefore, calls for experience-centered learning programs, not presentation-centered or materials-centered ones. You learn how to swim by swimming. You learn how to manage by managing. You learn how to use a computer by using a computer. Learning comes from doing the work itself, not from merely reading about it or from hearing someone else talk about it.

The cure to an over-Gutenbergized, left-brained learning culture is to immerse learners fully in a subject. Make their learning activity-based. Give them as authentic a real-world context as you can. Base their learning in experience (with feedback). Enable them to learn on many levels simultaneously. Involve their whole brain, their whole body, and all their senses in the learning.

You may very well need presentations and materials, but not as the centerpieces of your designs. The best designs are experience-based. You add presentations and materials only to initiate and support those experiences, not to be a substitute for them.

Accelerated Learning calls for experienced-based learning programs, not presentation- and materials-based ones.

Farewell to Harms

Clearly modern schooling and contemporary training can sometimes stifle and disable people and rob them of the joy of learning. It can keep them from exercising their full mind and realizing their full potential. But once you understand the cultural source of our learning dysfunctions, you can do something about it. You can begin to move education and training in the direction of greater health.

As a matter of fact, the whole aim of accelerated learning and of this book is to help people like yourself restore greater health and vitality to learning in schools, businesses, homes, everywhere. "All good learning," someone once said, "is therapy." To be an accelerated learning practitioner, then, is to be a kind of healer and therapist, restoring wholeness to the learning process and, thus, to the learners themselves.

Summary
The Educational Diseases of Western Civilization

THE DISEASE	THE SYMPTOMS	THE CURE
Puritanism	Serious, dreary, dry, rigorous and teacher-centered learning.	Learning that is joyful, nurturing, and learner-centered.
Individualism	Competition between learners. Isolation and disconnectedness.	Collaboration between learners in a learning community.
The Factory Model	One-size-fits all assembly line learning. Time-based and prescriptive.	A smorgasbord of options. Results-based and creative.
Western Scientific Thought	Linear, mechanistic, and compartmentalized approaches to learning.	Holistic, contextual, and interconnected approaches to learning.
Mind/Body Separation	Learning that is cognitive, verbal, left-brained, and physically passive.	Learning that is whole-brained, multisensory, and physically active.
Male Dominance	Emphasis on control, rational intelligence, and sequential processing.	Emphasis on nurture, whole-brain intelligence, and simultaneous processing.
The Printing Press	Words and abstract concepts as the foundation of learning.	Images and concrete experience as the foundation of learning.

PART 2

Natural Learning

CHAPTER 4

The Brain and Learning

Accelerated Learning is based on how people naturally learn. It finds in modern brain research helpful metaphors of how the brain learns, and it seeks to design effective "brain-based" learning environments accordingly.

There has been more brain research in the last 25 years than in all of human history combined. There is still much we don't know about the brain (and probably never will). But what we are discovering about the brain and learning seriously challenges many of our conventional educational beliefs and practices.

Brain Theories as Metaphors

All brain theories, of course, are oversimplifications. But they can serve as useful metaphors for helping us think about the complex organism of the brain in practical, concrete ways.

There are many views of the brain today, no one view giving us the whole picture by any means, but all views contributing to a richer understanding of how the brain learns. These views are not so much contradictory as complementary.

Here's one view: The brain is a chemical soup that communicates throughout all of its regions by manufacturing, distributing, and interacting with a myriad of different chemicals.

Here's another view: The brain is part of an electrical network of wiring that is distributed throughout the body and constantly sending and receiving messages. The amount of wiring is vast. The brain alone contains more than 100,000 miles of wiring. This wiring (called axons and dendrites) has millions of interactions a second with itself, with the network distributed

There has been more research into the brain and learning in the last 25 years than in all of human history combined.

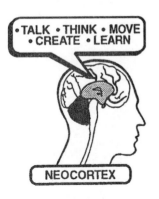

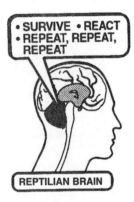

throughout the body, and with chemicals shipped through the blood stream.

And another view: The brain is a vast array of individual brain cells that form subsystems, which merge to form larger systems, which in turn merge to form even larger and more complex systems, which in turn merge to form even larger mega-systems— all interactive and all in touch with each other all the time.

Still another view: The brain is like a hologram where all parts contain the whole, and "memory" is distributed throughout the total system. When anything is truly learned, according to this theory, it is learned by the brain and body *as a whole*. The brain/body is a simultaneous processor, not a sequential one. It is designed to process total contexts or "gestalts," and not one isolated thing at a time.

The Theory of the Triune Brain

Another view of the brain that has gained popularity over the last 20 years is the theory of the Triune Brain ("triune" means "three in one"). According to this theory, the human brain can be thought of as having three separate (though interconnected) areas of specialization: The Reptilian Brain, the Limbic System, and the Neocortex.

Brain research is a fast-moving science and new discoveries are overturning old ones every day. So don't take any description of brain functioning (including this one) as absolute. There is certainly truth in the Triune Brain Theory, but this truth is unavoidably oversimplified and incomplete. Yet it has real value for us in understanding how the brain learns. Here's a brief description of the specialties of these three aspects of the brain according to the Triune Brain theory:

The Neocortex. This is the brain cap, the convoluted cover of grey matter that comprises about 80-85% of your brain mass. It is essential for many higher-level functions such as language, abstract thought, problem solving, forward planning, fine movement, and creativity. It's what makes us uniquely human.

The Limbic System. This is the midbrain that plays a big role in bonding and in emotions. It's the social and emotional brain. It also contains equipment essential for long-term memory.

The Reptilian Brain. This is the primal part of the brain (so named because reptiles have it too). Its major goal is survival (although it's not the only part of the brain concerned about this). It governs automatic functions like your heartbeat and circulatory system. It is the seat of instinctual, repetitive behavior and tends to follow precedent and routine blindly and ritualistically. It is believed to be the part of the brain involved in hierarchical power struggles. It knows how to deceive when necessary for its survival. It's an animal.

One Interconnected Brain

Again, the Triune Brain idea is an oversimplification. These three "brains" are interlinked in one total organism and often participate in each other's specialties in complex, subtle, and essential ways. It's best to think of these three aspects of the brain, then, not as physical locations, but as clearing houses for specialized functions. None of the three clearing houses works alone. All of them have relationships with the other clearing houses for help in fulfilling their functions. Vigorous amounts of sharing and exchange go on in the brain all the time.

> Nothing in the world is single
> All things by a law divine
> In one another's essence mingle.
> —Shelley

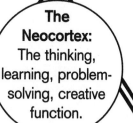

The Neocortex: The thinking, learning, problem-solving, creative function.

The Reptilian Brain: The instinctual, repetitive, animal survival function.

The Triune Brain

The Limbic System: The social, emotional, long-term memory function.

What's This Got to Do With Learning?

Everything. Traditional learning in the Industrial Age tended to emphasize the Reptilian functions: rote learning, repeat-after-me, the teacher as power center, the learner as passive obedient servant following a routine and precedent established by the hierarchy, a system driven by survival (the fear of failure), little concern with feelings and with social bonding in the educational setting, little effort to teach learners how to create, problem solve, and think on their own. (Too much independent thinking on the part of the learner, in fact, was considered subversive and a sign of insubordination.)

Using the Whole Brain for Learning

Today we need to use the powers of the total mind and the whole self for learning (mind, body, emotions, and all the senses). We know that using the *whole* brain is the key to making learning faster, more interesting, and more effective.

We certainly need to keep our **Reptilian function** alive with its survival instincts and automatic functions. Some obedience to precedent and routine is necessary and positive. But we need a lot more than that in order to be fully alive.

We need to involve the **Limbic function** in learning. Emotions, as research and common sense have verified, have a profound effect on the quality and quantity of learning. Positive feelings speed learning. (There is nothing that accelerates learning more than a sense of joy.) Negative feelings slow learning or stop it altogether. One of the major goals of the Preparation Phase of the Accelerated Learning Cycle is to create positive feelings in the learner. Another goal is to awaken the social intelligence of the Limbic system. Get learners to collaborate, rather than compete, say the researchers, and the learning will improve significantly.

And we need to fully exercise the **Neocortex function** of the brain if we want to optimize learning and human performance. We do this by teaching learners how to think for themselves, how to navigate (rather than store) information, how to learn,

Learning accelerates and deepens when the **whole** brain gets involved.

how to imagine, and how to create meaning and value for themselves out of information and experience.

Feelings Are Central

When feelings are positive and learners are in a relaxed, open state, they can "upshift" into the Neocortex (the learning brain). When feelings are negative and learners are stressed, they tend to "downshift" into the Reptilian brain with its concern not for learning but for survival. Learning then slows or comes to a screeching halt.

The Body Is the Mind; The Mind Is the Body

The brain and body are inseparably connected in a myriad of ways. Body movement, as an example, can improve brain functioning as Carla Hannaford points out in her book *Smart Moves: Why Learning Is Not All in Your Head*. And certain brain states can have a profound effect on the body.

Thinking, learning, and memory, after all, are not confined to your head, but are distributed throughout the body. Much thinking, learning, and decision making, for instance, takes place on the *cellular and molecular* level as Candice Pert points out in her book *The Molecules of Emotion*.

Traditional education has separated the body and the mind. It has treated learning as a "head" thing, as a rational, verbal process having little to do with the body with all its feelings and senses.

Because of this, we have tended to create learning environments that say to children (and adults): "Sit down, don't wiggle, and be quiet while you learn!" Rather, we should say, "Stand up, move around, and make noise while you learn!" Bodily movement stimulates the secretion of chemicals that are essential for neural network construction in the brain, and this aids learning.

Researchers discovered some time ago that functions like thinking and bodily movement are intimately connected in the

> Sitting still in confined places is one of the worst punishments that can be inflicted on the human species.
> Yet, this is what we require of students in school.
> —Edward T. Hall

brain. As an example, the part of your neocortex that governs thinking and problem solving lives right next door to the part of your neocortex that controls fine motor skills throughout your body. It's true to one degree or another for everybody that "If your body don't move, your brain don't groove."

The body and the mind are not two separate entities, but one totally integrated whole. In a very real sense, the mind is the body, and the body is the mind. The nervous system and the circulatory system tie them together as one.

Behaviorism and the Brain

Behaviorism was the reigning academic psychology in the United States for the greater part of the 20th century. As such, it has had a profound affect on corporate training.

According to what we now know about the brain, it is clear that Behaviorism had never been a whole-brain psychology but was, almost exclusively, the psychology of the Reptilian Brain.

Behaviorism had great insights into the Reptilian aspect of the brain, as far as they went. It's true that there is a part of us that is mechanical and ritualistic, that automatically responds to various external stimuli, and that can learn how to internalize and repeat various programmed behaviors. The problem with Behaviorism was that it presented itself (often quite dogmatically) as talking about the whole brain when it was dealing with only one aspect of it.

There is more to us than mechanistic, reptilian, stimulus/response functioning. But Behaviorism didn't address this. It had very little to say about social and emotional intelligence (the Limbic System), and less to say about creative and innovative thinking (the neocortex). And it took no interest at all in tapping into the wisdom hidden in the soul.

Training suffered as a result. People were taught how to react in a standard way, not how to think outside the box. Training became the programmed installation of controllable, repeatable, predictable, mechanical behaviors. "Performance Technology" (Behaviorism's new label) often does no better, although some

Behaviorism– the belief that all learning consists of a stimulus/response, carrot-and-stick training and that only observed behavior is worthy of study– has had a disastrous influence on 20th-century perceptions.

–A. Arnold
The Corrupted Sciences

performance technologists show signs that they are beginning to value the social, spiritual, emotional, creative, and systemic side of learning, and so are becoming less arrogantly prescriptive (i.e., Behavioristic).

The point is that we have to take what we can from Behaviorism and move beyond it into a psychology of learning that takes into account the whole brain and the whole social/emotional context of learning. This means, among other things, that we stop prescribing human performance (i.e., behaviors) and concentrate on results, encouraging people to constantly create ways of better achieving the results, and of achieving even *better* results.

We often confuse means and ends, as is shown by our use of the term "Performance Objective," a glaring oxymoron if ever there was one. Performance is a means, not an end in itself. It is a means by which some particular value can be created. The performance "means," then, need not be dogmatically prescribed, but can take all sorts of innovative forms, many of which can be created by the learners themselves.

Learning Is Life

It's true that all life is learning, but it's also true that, in a very real sense, all learning is life. Studies have indicated that people who continue to learn and mentally grow throughout their lives are much less likely to suffer from Alzheimer's disease. The brain can continually grow dendrites and new neural networks far into old age when stimulated with new learning challenges, as Cynthia Short points out in her brain exercise book for senior citizens, *Dendrites Are Forever*. The secrets of the fountain of youth, it seems, are exercise, the right diet, and continual learning.

The Implications of Brain Research for Learning

Modern theories of how the brain works are in conflict with many of our traditional assumptions about the brain and learning. These new theories, in fact, have deep and revolutionary implications for all education and training in Western culture. Here are just a few things you can do to assure that the learning programs you design and deliver are keeping pace with what we now know about the brain and learning

- Create learning environments that reduce stress and create positive feelings in people so they can "upshift" into their full learning brains.

- Provide people with problem-posing and information accessing exercises that stimulate them to think, make connections, build new neural networks, and create actionable meaning and value for themselves.

- Make learning social. Collaboration among learners engages more of the total brain and improves the quality and quantity of learning.

- Get people out of their seats and provide opportunities for physical movement and activity as part of the learning process.

- Delinearize and decompartmentalize information wherever you can and provide a total real-world context into which people can immerse their full selves and learn with all their senses on many levels simultaneously.

CHAPTER 5

The SAVI Approach to Learning

Activity-Based Learning (ABL)

Learning With the Whole Self

Activity-Based Learning (ABL) means getting physically active while you learn, using as many senses as possible, and getting your whole body/mind involved in the learning process.

Conventional training tends to keep people physically inactive for long periods of time. Brain paralysis sets in and learning slows to a creep or stops altogether. Getting people up and moving periodically awakens the body, improves circulation to the brain, and can have a positive impact on learning.

Activity-based learning is generally far more effective than presentation-based, materials-based, and media-based learning. And the reason for this is simple: *It gets the whole person totally involved.* It's been proven over and over again that people often learn more from well-chosen activities and experiences than they do from sitting in front of a presenter, a manual, a TV, or a computer.

Physical movement improves mental processing. The part of the human brain involved in bodily movement (the motor cortex) is tucked in right next to the part of the brain used for thinking and problem solving. To restrict bodily movement, then, is to hamper the mind from functioning at its best. On the other hand, to involve the body in learning tends to invoke one's full integrated intelligence.

If there is one thing
we should know
from years and years
of experience,
it's that
sleep learning
doesn't work.

Don't Just Sit There. Do Something.

Young children are such great learners because they use their whole bodies and all their senses to learn. Could you imagine a young child learning anything sitting in a lecture hall for a long stretch of time? What we fail to realize is that the same is true with most adults. Learning is always hampered when we separate the body and the mind, disregard the body, and appeal to rational consciousness alone as the gateway to the mind.

For many people, the mind falls asleep when there is no chance for some physical involvement. I'm like that myself. At *Training '99* in Chicago, I attended a keynote on how to make dynamic presentations. I fell stone cold asleep in the first 10 minutes. I wondered how many other people were glazing out, not because the presentation didn't have value, but because they were not allowed to move their bodies. Many learners find it hard to concentrate without doing something physical. (If their bodies don't move, their brains don't groove.) After years of observing unconscious audiences everywhere, I have come to the conclusion that *sleep learning doesn't work.*

The SAVI Approach to Learning

Learning doesn't automatically improve by having people stand up and move around. But combining physical movement with intellectual activity and the use of all the senses can have a profound effect on learning. I call this **SAVI** learning. The components are easy to remember.

1. **S**omatic: Learning by moving and doing

2. **A**uditory: Learning by talking and hearing

3. **V**isual: Learning by observing and picturing

4. **I**ntellectual: Learning by problem solving and reflecting

All four of these learning modes have to be present for optimal learning to occur. Since these elements are all integrated, the best kind of learning occurs when they are all used simultaneously.

Here's more detail on each of these four modes.

1. Somatic Learning

"Somatic" is from the Greek word for body— *soma* (as in *Psychosomatic*). It denotes tactile, kinesthetic, hands-on learning— getting physical and using and moving your body while you learn.

Bias Against the Body

Strong somatic learners, however, are at a disadvantage in Western culture, which has a long history of separating the body and the mind and disregarding the body as a vehicle for learning. According to the false belief of Western culture, learning involves the "head" alone and has nothing to do with what's below it. As a result, the "sit down, don't squirm, and shut up" approach to learning is the standard in schools and corporations.

The persecution of somatic learners continues to this day, and has even increased in the past 20 years. Children who are somatic, who can't sit still but who must move their bodies in order to keep their minds alive are often considered disruptive, learning disabled, and a menace to the system. They're labeled "hyperactive." And sometimes they are drugged.

But for many children hyperactivity is normal and healthy. It's their natural state of being. Yet, hyperactive children sometimes suffer because their schools don't have a clue what to do with them except to pronounce them abnormal and disabled.

Edward T. Hall, in his book *Beyond Culture*, complained about this way back in 1976.

> "The way children are treated in schools is sheer madness. Those who can't sit still are stuck with the hyperactive label and treated as anomalies and frequently drugged."

If your body don't move,
your brain don't groove.

Though Hall wrote these words 25 years ago, not much has changed. The bias against the body continues. There are currently about 5 million school children in the United States taking daily drugs for ADD (Attention Deficit Disorder) and ADHD (Attention Deficit Hyperactivity Disorder). Who said schools were drug-free zones? There is a legitimate ADD and ADHD condition that can and should be helped by drugs, but one recent study concluded that about 80% of the children now on school-administered drugs have been misdiagnosed. They are simply normal, healthy, hyperactive (i.e., physically active) kids.

The Body and the Mind Are One

Today, the mind/body split of Western culture and the prejudice against the use of the body in learning are being seriously challenged. Neurological research has exploded the false belief of Western culture that the mind and body are separate entities. Their findings indicate that the mind is distributed throughout the body. In essence, the body IS the mind. The mind IS the body. The two are one completely integrated electrical-chemical-biological system. So by inhibiting somatic learners from using their full physical bodies in learning, we are hampering the full function of their minds. (Perhaps in some cases it is the educational system that's learning disabled and not the individual learners at all.)

Two helpful books that report on some of the research into the body-mind connection are Carla Hannaford's *Smart Moves: Why Learning Is Not All in Your Head* and Candice Pert's *The Molecules of Emotion*.

Getting the Body Involved

In order to stimulate the mind-body connection, create learning events that get people up and out of their seats and physically active from time to time. Not all learning needs to be physically active, but by alternating between physically active and physically passive learning activities you can help everyone's learning. Here are some examples of how you can get learners *physically* involved in the learning.

People can take roles as props and components to actively simulate such things as:

- Spreadsheets
- Telephone networks
- The workings of a piece of equipment
- Computer screens and applications
- Structures and functions in the human body
- Structures and functions in nature
- Chemical reactions
- Processes in manufacturing
- Business procedures
- The features and benefits of a product
- Language, grammar, syntax
- Episodes in history
- Histograms and other statistical tools
- Sales or communication processes

People can get physical while they:

- Build a model of a process or procedure
- Physically manipulate components of a process or system
- Create large pictograms and peripherals
- Act out a process, system, or set of concepts
- Have an experience, then talk about and reflect on it
- Complete a project that requires physical activity
- Do an active learning exercise (a simulation, a learning game, etc.)
- Take a field trip. Then write, draw, and talk about what was learned
- Interview people outside the class
- In teams, create active learning exercises for the whole class

2. Auditory Learning

Our auditory minds are stronger than we realize. Our ears continually capture and store auditory information, even without our conscious awareness. And when we make our own sounds by talking, several significant areas of our cerebrum are activated.

Before Johannes Gutenberg invented the printing press in the 1440s, most information was transmitted from generation to generation auditorially. The epics and myths and tales of all ancient cultures were passed down through oral tradition: *Beowulf*, Homer's *Iliad* and *Odyssey*, *Gilgamesh*, and countless more. And, as you can imagine, they were told with a dramatic, emotional and auditory richness that added to their memorability.

The ancient Greeks encouraged people to learn out loud by dialog. Their philosophy was: If you want to learn more about anything, talk about it nonstop. Auditory learning was the standard for all cultures as far back in history as we can go.

The Gutenberg Revolution

After Gutenberg's invention became widely used and people were becoming literate, everyone read out loud. They could not imagine receiving information without an auditory component. As time wore on, the auditory gradually evaporated to the point where our "Silence Please" libraries now discourage sound altogether.

But all learners (particularly strong auditory ones) learn by sounds, by dialog, by reading out loud, by telling someone out loud what they just experienced, heard, or learned, by talking to themselves, by remembering jingles and rhymes, by listening to audio cassettes, and by repeating sounds in their heads.

Bringing Back the Auditory

The need to bring the dialog and the sound back into learning is reflected in a recent Dr. Seuss book, *Hooray for Diffendoofer Day*. It's all about a school that seeks to be effective by reversing some of the learning inhibitors that have plagued traditional education in the Industrial Age. The librarian, for instance, believes in restoring the auditory to learning.

> Miss Loon is our librarian,
> She hides behind the shelves,
> And often cries out, "LOUDER!"
> When we're reading to ourselves.

In designing courses that appeal to the strong auditory channels in people, look for ways to get learners to talk about what they are learning. Have them translate experience into sound. Ask them to read out loud— dramatically if they wish. Get them to talk out loud while they solve problems, manipulate models, gather information, make action plans, master skills, review learning experiences, or create personal meanings for themselves.

Here is a brief list of starter ideas for increasing the use of the auditory in learning.

- Have learners read out loud from manuals and computer screens.

- Have learners read materials a paragraph at a time paraphrasing each paragraph into a tape recorder. Then ask them to listen to the tape several times for reinforcement.

- Ask learners to create their own audio tape of key words, processes, definitions, or procedures.

- Tell learners stories that have the learning material embedded in them.

- Have learners in pairs describe to each other in detail what they just learned and how they are going to apply it.

- Ask learners to practice a skill or perform a function while describing out loud in great detail what they're doing.

- Have learners create a rap, rhyme or auditory mnemonic out of what they are learning.

- Ask learners in groups to talk nonstop when doing creative problem solving or long-term planning. (The conversations can be recorded to capture the ideas.)

3. Visual Learning

Visual acuity, although more pronounced in some people than others, is strong in everyone. The reason is because there is more equipment in everyone's head for processing visual information than any other sense.

Several years ago I was given a grant from the U.S. Government to study the effects of mental imagery on learning. My colleague, Dr. Owen Caskey of Texas Tech University, and I found that the people who used imagery to learn technical and scientific information did, on average, 12% better on immediate recall than those who did not use imagery, and 26% better on long-term retention. And this statistic held for everyone regardless of age, ethnicity, gender, or preferred learning style.

Helping Learners See the Point

It helps everyone (particularly the visual learner) to "see" what a presenter or book or computer program is talking about. Visual learners learn best when they can see real-world examples, diagrams, idea maps, icons, pictures, and images of all kinds while they are learning.

And sometimes they learn even better when they create their own idea maps, diagrams, icons, and images out of what they are learning. When seventh and eighth graders in New Jersey were asked to create large mural-size pictograms out of their homework, both their learning and their interest went up.

It helps adults also to create pictograms, icons, or three-dimensional table-top displays, and other visuals out of their learning material. One organization, seeking to reinforce certain operational procedures in a factory, had the machine operators themselves create their own colorful icons, pictograms, and job aids that they then displayed around the shop floor and on their machines.

Another technique that works for everyone, especially for people with strong visual skills, is to ask them to *observe* a real-world situation and then to think and talk about it, drawing out

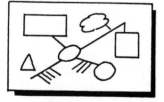

> You can observe a lot just by watching.
>
> –Yogi Berra

the processes, principles, or meanings that it illustrated.

> **Here are a few more things you can use to make learning more visual.**
>
> - Picturesque language (metaphors, analogies)
> - Vivid presentation graphics
> - 3-dimensional objects
> - Dramatic body language
> - Vivid stories
> - Pictogram creation (by learners)
> - Icon job aids
> - Field observations
> - Colorful decorations
> - Room peripherals
> - Mental imagery exercises

4. Intellectual Learning

We really have to define this one. By "Intellectual," I don't mean an emotionless, disconnected, rationalistic, "academic" and compartmentalized approach to learning.

For me the word "Intellectual" indicates what learners do in their minds internally as they exercise their intelligence to reflect on experience and to create connections, meanings, plans, and values out of it. It's the reflecting, creating, problem-solving, and meaning-building part of a person.

The Intellectual (according to the way I'm using the term) is the sense maker of the mind; the means by which the human being "thinks," integrates experience, creates new neural networks, and learns. It connects the body's mental, physical, emotional, and intuitive experiences together to build fresh meaning for itself. It's the means by which the mind turns experience into knowledge, knowledge into understanding, and understanding (we hope) into wisdom.

When a learning exercise, no matter how clever it is, does not sufficiently challenge this intellectual side of a learner, the exercise will appear to many to be shallow and childish. This happens with some "creative" techniques that get people physically moving (S) and have strong auditory (A) and visual (V) input, but lack intellectual depth (I). You end up with learning that is "SAV," a superficial gloss that is bound to wash off in the first full rain of reality.

But when the Intellectual side of learning is engaged, most people can accept even the most playful learning exercise without feeling that it's shallow, childish, or trite.

The Intellectual aspect of learning gets exercised when you have learners engage in activities such as:

- Solving problems
- Analyzing experiences
- Doing strategic planning
- Generating creative ideas
- Accessing and distilling information
- Formulating questions
- Creating mental models
- Applying new ideas to the job
- Creating personal meaning
- Thinking through the implications of an idea

S-A-V-I: Putting It All Together

Learning is optimized when all four SAVI components are present in a single learning event. For example, people can learn something by watching a presentation (V), but they can learn much more if they can do something while it is going on (S), talk about what they are learning (A), and think through how to apply the information being presented to their job (I). Or they can enhance their problem-solving skills (I) if they are simultaneously manipulating something (S) to produce a pictogram or 3-dimensional display (V) while they talk out loud about what they are doing (A).

Chapters in this book that have an "Examples from the Field" section in them will give you other ideas of what you can do to create SAVI learning experiences for people.

PART 3

The Four Phases of Learning

CHAPTER 6

A Summary of the Four Phases

The Four Phase Learning Cycle

All human learning can be thought of as having four components:

1. **Preparation**
   (the *arousal* of interest)

2. **Presentation**
   (the initial *encounter* of new knowledge or skill)

3. **Practice**
   (the *integration* of the new knowledge or skill)

4. **Performance**
   (the *application* of the new knowledge and skill to real-world situations)

Unless all four components are present in one form or another, no real learning occurs.

A Universal Model

This simple 4-part process is universal. It applies to all learning, everywhere, always. It applies to babies learning to play with toys, children learning to ride bicycles, teenagers learning a foreign language, adults learning how to dance, people learning computers, employees learning how to be successful managers— everything.

Subverting the Human Learning Process

Violating the learning process is a widespread practice in schools and businesses today. When any one of the four stages is not present, learning deteriorates or stops completely. Here's how.

Four Ways the Wheel of Learning Can Go Flat

No Arousal

Weak Preparation Phase

Learning is subverted when people are not open and ready to learn, don't see the benefit of the learning for themselves, have no interest, or are hampered by learning barriers. In terms of barriers, many people harbor subconscious negative feelings about learning. Based on their past experience, they may associate formal learning situations with incarceration, boredom, irrelevance, the fear of humiliation, and stress. When these barriers are not overcome, accelerated and effective learning is stopped cold right at the door.

No Encounter

Weak Presentation Phase

Learning is subverted when people do not encounter new knowledge and skill in ways that are meaningful to them and that engage their full selves. When they are treated as passive consumers and not active creators in the learning process, their learning just hobbles along or comes to a screeching halt. The same thing occurs when a person's personal learning style is not addressed somehow in the presentation phase. For instance, people who have to move and be active while they learn will not learn much at all during a long instructor-led presentation unless they are given something to do.

No Integration

Weak Practice Phase

Learning is subverted when people are not given sufficient time to integrate new knowledge and skill into their current structure of self, into their internal organization of meaning, beliefs, and skills. You'll hear this repeated many times in this book: It is what the *learner* says and does that is more important than what the instructor or the instructional media says and does for the actual learning. Learning is not telling, whether the teller is a person or a computer. Learning is not an act of consumption but an act of production on the part of the learner. Knowledge is not something a learner absorbs. Knowledge is something a learner creates. Learners need time for integration.

Weak Performance Phase

Learning is subverted when people do not have a chance to immediately apply what they've learned. Without immediate application of the newly learned knowledge and skill to the real world, much of it evaporates. Poof! It's gone! Cold storage learning has never worked (e.g., "Remember this bit of information. You may need it in six months.") One study discovered that without immediate application and reinforcement, only about 5% of classroom learning stuck. But with immediate application and the proper coaching and support, 90% survived.

No Application

Twisted Priorities

Conventional training has tended to emphasize the Presentation Phase (Phase 2) over all other phases of the learning cycle. As an example, when designing a learning program we often put 80% or more of our effort, money, and time into creating presentation materials (student workbooks, PowerPoint presentations, computer programs, and the like). Yet the Preparation Phase accounts for, at very best, only about 20% of the learning. And it's almost completely useless unless preceded by a Presentation phase and followed by healthy Practice and Performance phases.

This prejudice toward a bloated Phase 2 stems from the false belief that teaching is telling and learning is observing. For some people at some times that might be true, but for most people most of the time, learning is a matter of trial, feedback, reflection, and retrial. The Presentation Phase exists only to initiate the learning process, not to be the center piece of it.

Get your priorities straight, and learning will improve. Give less attention to the Presentation Phase and more balanced attention to the other three phases, and accelerated, enhanced learning will result. This book urges you to create experience-based (not presentation-based or materials-based) learning programs. People learn more from experience than they do from presentations and materials. The presentations and materials are there simply to initiate and support active learning experiences, nothing more.

Full 4-Phase Learning

Following in this book is a chapter on each of the four phases of learning with tips, techniques, and tactics for each. For now, here is a brief overview of some of the things you can do to support learning in each of the four phases.

Phase 1: Preparation

The Goal of the Preparation Phase is to arouse learners' interest, give them positive feelings about the forthcoming learning experience, and put them into an optimal state for learning. You do this through:

- positive suggestions
- learner benefit statements
- clear, meaningful goals
- curiosity raising
- creating a positive physical environment
- creating a positive emotional environment
- creating a positive social environment
- calming people's fears
- removing learning barriers
- raising questions and posing problems
- arousing people's curiosity
- getting people fully involved from the start

Phase 2: Presentation

The Goal of the Presentation Phase is to help the learners encounter the new learning material in ways that are interesting, enjoyable, relevant, multisensory, and that appeal to all learning styles. You do this through:

- collaborative pretests and knowledge sharing
- observations of real-world phenomenon
- whole-brain, whole-body involvement
- interactive presentations
- colorful presentation graphics and props
- variety to appeal to all learning styles
- partner- and team-based learning projects
- discovery exercises (personal, partnered, team-based)
- real-world, contextual learning experiences
- problem-solving exercises

Phase 3: Practice

The Goal of the Practice Phase is to help learners integrate and incorporate the new knowledge or skill in a variety of ways. You do this through:

- learner processing activities
- hands-on trial/feedback/reflection/retrial
- real-world simulations
- learning games
- action learning exercises
- problem-solving activities
- individual reflection and articulation
- partner- and team-based dialog
- collaborative teaching and review
- skill-building practice activities
- teachbacks

Phase 4: Performance

The Goal of the Performance Phase is to help learners apply and extend their new knowledge or skill to the job so that the learning sticks and performance continually improves. You do this through:

- immediate real-world application
- creating and executing action plans
- follow-through reinforcement activities
- post-session reinforcement materials
- on-going coaching
- performance evaluation and feedback
- peer support activities
- supportive organizational and environmental changes

> More details on the four phases follow
> with a wealth of ideas for each.

CHAPTER 7

Phase 1:
Preparation Techniques

The Preparation Phase has to do with preparing the learner to learn. It's the essential first step in learning. Without it, learning slows or comes to a complete halt altogether. Yet, in the rush to "cover the material" we often neglect this phase to the detriment of good learning.

Learner prep is like preparing the soil for the seed. When we do it properly, we create the conditions for healthy growth.

Why Learner Prep?

The aim of learner preparation is to

1. Get learners out of a passive or resistant mental state.

2. Remove learning barriers.

3. Arouse learners' interest and curiosity.

4. Give learners positive feelings about, and a meaningful relationship with, the subject matter.

5. Create active learners who are inspired to think, learn, create, and grow.

6. Get people out of isolation and into a learning community.

Removing Learning Barriers

Learners can approach a learning situation with all sorts of conscious and unconscious blocks that inhibit learning. Here are a few of them:

- No sense of personal benefit
- Fear of failure or social embarrassment
- Fear of change and personal growth

BARRIER REMOVAL

- Indifference to the subject matter
- Hostility toward the subject matter
- Forced attendance
- Personal problems and distractions
- A sense of "I already know this stuff."
- A feeling of impending boredom

These and other blocks can cause stress, brain numbing, and a severe reduction in learning ability. Removing or reducing these blocks will result in improved learning ability every time.

The Components of Learner Prep

There are many elements that go into preparing learners for a learning experience. Here are some of the major ones:

1. Positive suggestions
2. A positive physical environment
3. Clear, meaningful goals
4. Learner benefits
5. Pre-course learner prep kit
6. A positive social environment
7. Total learner involvement
8. Curiosity arousal

Even though all these elements are interrelated and work together, let's explore them one at a time.

> The first task of any learning program is to get the learners aroused, open, and ready to learn.

1. Positive Suggestions

Many people have negative feelings about learning. Their unconscious memories associate formal learning with pain, stress, humiliation, incarceration— who knows what. Unless they replace these negative suggestions (i.e. assumptions) with positive ones, their learning will be hampered.

That is because our assumptions tend to color (and even create) our experience. Negative assumptions tend to create negative experience. Positive assumptions tend to create positive experience.

Sometimes facilitators unwittingly sabotage learning by putting negative suggestions into the environment, saying things like:

- We've got a ton of material to cover and not much time.

- This is a very complex, difficult subject.

- I know this is boring, but stay with it.

- If you don't learn this, you won't have a job.

- You've got to remember these eight steps.

- This may not make sense to you, but try to learn it.

Arrgh! Talk about crippling the learning process! Where is the joy of learning in all of this? Facilitators need to be sensitive to the negative suggestions that they may be putting into the environment and replace them with positive ones. The language of positive suggestion speaks to the whole person— conscious and paraconscious— and thus can have a profound effect on learning outcomes. Here are just a few examples of positive suggestions:

- After you master this material, you'll be able to...

- You'll find this fun and interesting.

- This is going to be extremely valuable for you.

- You'll love what you'll be able to do with this.

- Boy, are you in for a treat!

- This is going to help you so much you'll be astonished.

- Learning this is a piece of cake.

- I know you're going to be successful in learning this because we've seen people like you master this material before quite easily and it's made a positive difference in their lives.

A positive feeling toward the learning experience is the necessary first step in learning.

Positive suggestions should not strike one as silly, superficial, unbelievable, or frivolous, but should be realistic, honest, matter-of-fact, and to the point. In any event, when you set the mind for positive outcomes, more than likely positive outcomes will be what you get. When you help people replace their negative assumptions with positive ones, a sense of enjoyment and relevance floods in to accelerate their learning.

2. A Positive Physical Environment

Suggestions, either positive or negative, are made by the learning environment itself. The standard 19th-century classroom arrangement of rows and aisles in a stark setting often makes negative suggestions, reminding people of painful and dehumanizing experiences they may have had in similar environments. A typical classroom can suggest military regimentation, teacher-centered control, mechanistic learning, boredom, incarceration, and learning as a process of absorbing someone else's information rather than creating your own knowledge.

If the physical environment inspires negative feelings and reminds people (consciously or unconsciously) of negative, dehumanizing experiences, you can be sure that it will have a negative impact on the learning.

You don't want a learning environment to resemble a traditional classroom, but to have a happy, positive, stimulating feel to it— one that inspires positive associations and happy feelings in people. Anything you can do to get away from the feel and look of the standard classroom is bound to help relax and energize people.

There are many ways of doing this. Clustered seating, rather than rows and aisles, can help de-stress and rehumanize the environment. Or you could divide the space into functional areas: theater seating for presentations, round tables for collaborative activities, work stations for various learning exercises, etc.

And you could decorate the learning space with what we call

peripherals. A peripheral is anything in the environment that adds color, beauty, interest, and stimulation and contains, where possible, information relative to the course. You don't want to overdo it, and different audiences and different subject matters may require different sets of peripherals, but here's a few ideas of what you might provide.

Some Suggestions

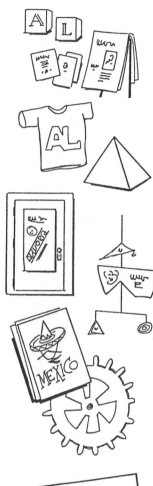

- Wall hangings
- Velcro boards
- Magnetic boards
- Flannelgraphs
- Plants
- Tabletop displays
- Mock-ups
- Toys
- Candles
- Large information graphs
- Mobiles
- Decorations of all kinds
- Flowers
- Floor displays
- Equipment displays
- Supplemental resources
- Instructor costumes
- Colorful tablecloths

Course themes, when used, will give you ideas for room arrangement and peripherals. People have decorated rooms like beaches, hospital emergency rooms, law courts, athletic stadiums, picnic groves, cruise ships, and on and on.

Music in the form of CDs, cassettes, and music videos can warm the environment and be used during breaks, for concert reviews, and during certain learning exercises. Chapter 11 on *Music for Learning* has more information about how you can use music as an aid to learning in the classroom.

Aromas in the room (as long as you don't overdo it) can help make a positive environment. Aromatherapists claim that citrus aromas promote mental alertness and that vanilla and lavender aromas are calming. See Chapter 18 for more detail.

One Caveat: A colorful, stimulating room by itself is not enough. The other components of accelerated learning must be present also, or the whole thing could backfire on you and be a big waste of time.

3. Clear, Meaningful Goals

Learners need a clear idea of what the purpose of a course is and what they will be able to do (or to be) as a result. You can spell this out with words, pictures, examples, demonstrations, or anything that makes the goals clear and concrete for the learners.

And it helps to warm your goals up so that they speak to the hearts as well as to the minds of the learners. Traditional behavioral objectives sometimes sound cold, "academic," distant, ritualistic, and mechanical— as in this example:

> Terminal Objective: At the end of this training you will be able to splice the CFW line to the Q-Bar mechanism in under a 30-minute time frame with no more than a 2% error rate based on the Seuben-Cranach Analyzer. The Enabling Objectives for this are…

Holy obfuscation! I don't even know what a CFW line is, let alone a Seuben-Cranach Analyzer. And this is supposed to warm me up? Really, is there a better way to do this? Can you eliminate some of the jargon, present the big picture, and bring some meaningful relevance into the situation? Objectives need not sound cold, mechanical, and menacing to be clear and effective. Quite the opposite. In the movie *Dead Poets Society* when Mr. Keating was preparing his class of high school boys for a course in poetry, he took them into the hall, had them read a few lines of Whitman, interpreted it as *Carpe Diem* (Latin for "Seize the day!") and, while they bent in close to observe the pictures of earlier graduates, now deceased, whispered in a dramatic voice:

> "Carpe Diem! Seize the day, boys!
> Make your life extraordinary."

Now there's a goal you can get your life around— not to read and analyze poems to get a grade, but to use poetry as an aid to building a fully alive, extraordinary, and successful life. The goal of the poetry class had been humanized into something warm, touchable, relevant, and deeply motivational.

It's common for us to sometimes confuse ends and means and to think we're describing goals when we're just describing means. To avoid this kind of goal confusion, state any learning objective that you currently have and ask "Why?" two or three times to get closer to the real goal of the learning.

In this way, you'll discover that goals are not things like learning how to use Excel, or how to coach someone, or how to sell, but how to be more effective, fulfilled, and successful.

Learners themselves can help each other focus and clarify goals in a meaningful way. Later on in this chapter you'll see some examples.

4. Learner Benefits

There is a fine line between goals and benefits, but goals tend to be related to the "what," while benefits are related to the "why." Learners learn best when they know why they're learning and can appreciate how the learning has relevance and value for them personally. People learn for personal payoffs. If they don't see any payoffs, why should they learn?

It's therefore essential right at the start to use benefits to get people connected with the subject in positive ways.

Learner benefits might fall into some of the following general categories.

- Reduce pain
- Increase pleasure
- Save time or money
- Make life easier
- Increase happiness
- Stay current and viable
- Get refreshed and renewed
- Become more effective
- Improve personal satisfaction
- Improve personal status
- Improve self-image
- Increase income
- Help create a better world or workplace

How many of these benefits do you emphasize in your programs? And what other benefits are there that might get learners excited, open, and ready to learn?

People learn for the payoffs. Where there is no sense of payoff, there can be no sustained accelerated learning.

5. Pre-Course Learner Prep Kit

In many cases learner preparation can begin before the learning program starts. When appropriate, learners can be sent a pre-course kit that can contain a smorgasbord of items to aid in getting them ready to learn. The kit can help allay fears, specify goals, clarify benefits, raise curiosity and interest, and create positive feelings about the upcoming learning experience.

A learner prep kit could contain any or all of the following items:

- A brief cover letter

- An agenda in verbal form

- An agenda in picture form

- A pamphlet on how to get the most out of the program

- A booklet containing goals, positive suggestions, learner benefits, and testimonials from previous attendees

- An audio tape containing the same information as in the booklet

- A camcorded videotape of the same

- An object related to course content

- A list of questions that will be used in an opening quiz game

- A list of information to gather prior to the start of the learning program

- A questionnaire to be completed prior to the class

A course theme might suggest other items and materials for the kit. For instance, if you're using a journey theme, people might receive a passport and course outline in the form of an itinerary. If you're using a baseball theme, people might receive a ticket to the game and a scorecard.

The mind is not
a vessel to be filled
but a fire to be ignited.

–Plutarch

6. A Positive Social Environment

To help prepare people for an optimal learning experience, create a collaborative environment right from the start. Get people out of isolation and into a genuine learning community and you will help their learning measurably.

Collaboration helps learners reduce their stress and use more of their psychic energy for learning (rather than for competition and self-protection). Collaboration among learners creates the human synergy that allows for the free flow of insights, ideas, and information. And it enhances the learning experience for everyone.

Linking is the essence of intelligence, whether in the brain, the classroom, or the workplace. The more people link their knowledge and insights with each other, the smarter everyone becomes.

Western civilization, with its excessive emphasis on individualism, has often destroyed the social nature of learning, creating instead learning environments that disconnect people from each other. The effect of this on the actual long-term learning is often negative.

In contrast, research confirms the positive effects that collaboration has on learning. A study at the University of Minnesota using computers as the learning vehicle discovered that when two people share a computer and their experience is structured so that they dialog about what they're learning and help each other, the quantity and quality of learning goes up for both of them. Bunny Howard of Florida Community College, using the same technique, was able to speed learning by a factor of three. Bell Atlantic, Travelers Insurance, and many other organizations have experienced significant jumps in learning using the collaborative approach.

It's important to build a learning community right from the start. You could begin a learning program with a collaborative activity related to introductions, goals, learner benefits, or knowledge assessment.

> Linking is the essence of intelligence.

You could begin with a collaborative pretest, or a team-based information scavenger hunt, or a Jeopardy game, or a team-based learning project or problem-solving exercise— anything to get people into the learning material with each other.

People should feel from the start that they are not in social isolation but in a caring community where everyone takes responsibility for everyone else and everyone is a teacher and a learner simultaneously. If you do nothing else but get people collaborating with each other, learning will improve for everyone.

7. Total Learner Involvement

It's important to get learners totally involved and to get them involved totally. Learning is not a spectator sport, but a highly participatory one.

Learning, after all, is not the passive absorption of information, but the active creation of knowledge and skill. Learning is completely up to the learner and is not the responsibility of the designer or the facilitator. The designer and facilitator are responsible for setting the table with appetizing and nourishing dishes, but it's the learner's responsibility to eat.

To provide everything for learners and then spoon-feed them is bad for both the facilitator and the learners. It makes the facilitator subject to burnout and the learners subject to passivity and torpor.

A facilitator who is always jabbering and always hovering over a learner is a serious menace to the learning process. The facilitator's role is to initiate the learning process and then get out of the way. The sacred vow of every learning facilitator should be "No Spoon-feeding!"

The facilitator's role
is to initiate the
learning process
and then
get out of the way.
–John Warren

It's what the learners say and do that is more important for learning than what the facilitator says and does. The facilitator's main role, then, is to get *learners* to say and to do— to get them totally involved in their own learning.

8. Curiosity Arousal

One of the aims of learner prep is to get learners into a natural childlike state where their innate ability for learning can take over. The childlike state is characterized by openness, freedom, fearlessness, joy, and *a driving sense of curiosity*.

Arousing a learner's curiosity goes a long way in getting the learner open and ready to learn. Learning (and life itself) stagnates when there is nothing more to be curious about. The saddest thing any human being could think or say is, "I've seen it all, I've heard it all, I know it all." At that point their effective life stops. But spark people's curiosity and you bring them back to life, and you get them ready to become more than they were before— which is the essence of all good learning. Then they can search new paths, make new discoveries, learn new skills, and become growing and developing human beings again.

You can raise people's curiosity in many ways. Here are just a few ways of doing it:

- Give people problems to solve in teams.
- Send partners on fact-finding missions.
- Play question/answer games.
- Have people create questions or pose problems for each other.
- Engage learners in self-discovery learning projects of all kinds.

Wonder is the seed of
knowledge.
–Francis Bacon

Idea Treasure Chest
For the Preparation Phase

1. Hold an open house prior to a course where people can meet each other, observe the learning materials, and even help decorate the room.

2. Give learners a series of questions to answer before coming to class and ask them to interview, or tag along with, experienced graduates to get the answers.

3. Ask past graduates of a learning program to visit or call people who are about to attend, sharing some of the benefits of the program with them and answering any questions they might have about it.

4. Before a program, assign people to teams and give them a task to perform prior to the start of the program. You could ask them to research a topic, solve a problem, answer a series of questions, do a survey, create a set of learning goals for their team, or create pretest questions for the class.

5. Call learners ahead of time, welcoming them to the program and reviewing some of the benefits they'll derive from it.

6. Prior to a program, send people one or more e-mail messages with positive suggestions about the program and a review of its goals and benefits.

7. Send learners a list of quotations relative to a program or a review of its key concepts and ask them to make (and bring with them to class) a large colorful banner, poster, or sign for the classroom containing one of the quotations or key concepts.

Goal Setting

1. As people arrive for a learning program, give them a large index card and ask them to write on it their main goal or goals in attending the program. As an icebreaker, ask everyone to mingle, introduce themselves to each other, and share their goals.

2. As an add-on to 1, ask people with the same or very similar goals to form a group. Ask each group to elect a

spokesperson. Ask each spokesperson to tell the class what the main goal of their group is and why.

3. Put the learning objectives on flipcharts, one per flipchart, and post them on the wall. Ask learners to rise and sign or put a check mark on those flipcharts that contain the most important goals for them personally. Debrief.

4. Give learners two or three large cards. Ask them to write on each card a goal or an expectation they have for the learning program, signing their name to each card. Then have them post the cards on a wall in the room. (You can group the cards by goal type if you wish.) Throughout the learning program as one of their goals is achieved or one of their expectations is met, ask them to remove that card from the wall. What remains is what is still to be worked on.

5. Using tape, roll paper, or yarn, create a long continuum on the wall or on the floor, labeling one end "Important" and the other end "Unimportant." As you read each learning or performance objective of the program, ask people to stand at that position on the continuum that represents their feelings of the importance of that objective for them. Ask questions and dialog about this as appropriate after each objective.

6. Put people in small teams. Ask each team to create a colorful pictogram on a flipchart representing what each member of their team hopes to derive from the learning program. Then have each team post their pictogram on the wall and review their goals with the whole group.

7. Put a huge peripheral of a genie on the wall. Give each learner three large Post-It notes. Ask them to write one wish they have for the learning program on each Post-It note and post their three wishes on or next to the genie. Discuss as appropriate.

8. Ask people to complete and sign a learning contract prior to the start of a program that guides them in specifying what outcomes they want and what they are prepared to do to to achieve those outcomes.

9. Ask people to come to class with a colorful peripheral they can hang on the wall that represents what they want to be, feel, and be able to do as a result of the learning program.

Positive Suggestions

1. Ask past participants to come to your class at the beginning and tell the learners how the program has benefited them.

2. As people arrive, give each of them their graduation certificate. Ask them to put it in a safe place. Tell them that you will sign it at the end of the program when they have mastered the learning material, which they are bound to do.

3. Have a display of success stories in the room. The display could have pictures of past participants with statements in their own words of how the learning program has contributed to their success on the job.

4. Record a video of "testimonials" from previous attendees praising the class and relating what they've been able to accomplish as a result. Show the video at the start of the new class.

5. Have learners recall their best learning experience and tell the group what they can do to make this new learning experience just like it.

6. At the end of a program ask the class to create a time capsule for the next class. Ask them to write positive suggestions and encouraging words about the program on cards. Put the cards in a tube or box and seal it. At the start of a new class, break the time capsule open, distribute the cards, and have the learners read them out loud to the group.

Barrier Removal

1. Ask people to put all their fears, barriers, and reservations about the new learning on cards and read the cards to the group as they drop them into a mock casket or "suspend" them for the time being in a bucket hanging from the ceiling.

2. Put people in small teams. Give each team a barrier that a learner might have about the new learning. Ask them to come up with three or more suggestions for overcoming this barrier. Then have each team review their suggestions with the group.

3. Have the learners post their positive feelings about the learning program on one flipchart and their negative feelings on another. Then debrief with the whole group.

4. Give everyone an index card. Ask them to write on it a barrier they might have about the new learning. Ask everyone to rise, mingle around the room, find a partner, and exchange cards. Then have partners counsel each other, making

suggestions to each other about how the barrier might be removed. Debrief with the whole class as appropriate.

5. Give everyone a large empty cardboard box covered with butcher paper to look like a concrete block. Ask each person to write on his or her block a major barrier they might have to achieving the goals of the course. (The barrier could reside in them or in the work environment.) Ask them to build a wall out of their "blocks." Then ask the group to come up with suggestions for removing each block in turn. If the group agrees that the suggestion will work, the block is removed.

A Positive Physical Environment

1. Ask learners to bring something to the room to beautify and humanize the learning environment: flowers, plants, pictures of their children, prints and other peripherals for the wall, kites to hang from the ceiling, whatever.

2. As an icebreaker, ask learners to take 10 minutes and help you rearrange the room and decorate it with the peripherals you have provided.

3. In a computer class for neophytes, put two people to a computer. With craft materials you have provided, ask learners to make colorful costumes for their computers and to give their computers crazy names. Then as they introduce themselves, each pair can introduce their computer as well, telling the group what they want it to do for them.

4. In multiweek classes, have a different theme for each week. Make a different team responsible for the decorations each week.

5. Have each class make a huge colorful mural of what they have learned in the class. Leave the murals up for subsequent classes as an introduction and a review.

Learner Benefits

1. Put people in teams. Give each team one of the objectives of the class. Ask them to come up with as many benefits of achieving that objective as they can think of and present their findings to the group.

2. Make large wall posters of each of the major learner benefits of the class. Ask people to stand by the benefit that is most important to them. Ask them to explain why.

3. Give each person a piece of paper and ask them to write on the top of it a major benefit people can expect as a result of the new learning. Then have people mingle to get as many signatures on their benefit statement as they can from people who think it's important. Dialog about this as appropriate.

4. Put people in a circle. Have people toss a Koosh ball around. Whoever catches it has to describe one benefit people will get from the learning program.

5. Go around the room at random and ask everyone to complete this sentence: "The greatest benefit I'm going to get out of this program is…"

Creating a Learning Community

1. Give learners a pretest, asking them to use each other and anything they can find in the room as resources in answering the questions.

2. Put people in teams. Send each team on a 20-item scavenger hunt for information relative to the subject matter of the program. See which team can retrieve all the items of information first.

3. Put people in teams. Give each team a problem to solve relative to the learning program. Have teams report their findings to the group.

4. Have everyone select a learning partner at the start. Change learning partners periodically throughout the program.

5. As people arrive for class, give everyone a card with either a term or a definition of a term on it (or a card with either a question or an answer on it). Ask people to find their counterpart. This is their first partner. As partners introduce themselves, ask them to share their term and definition (or their question and answer) with the group.

6. Make several poster board puzzles, each containing a question to answer or a problem to solve relative to the learning material. Make one puzzle for each team you plan to have. Cut each puzzle into the number of members you want in each team. Jumble all the puzzle pieces together. As people arrive, ask each person to select a puzzle piece. Then, as an icebreaker, have people find their teammates by putting the pieces together into complete puzzles. Then have the teams answer the question or solve the problem that's on their puzzle, reporting their results to the whole group.

Examples from the Field

Some Positive Physical Environments

A major U.S. airline brought 15 of its management trainers together for two days to brainstorm ideas for a new management training program. The room assigned for the meeting was sterile and depressing— hardly a place to inspire creativity. So to properly prepare people for doing out-of-the-box thinking, the trainers removed all the ugly corporate furniture and transformed the room into "Brainstorm Beach." These pictures, both taken from the same spot, show the room before and after the transformation. Where would *you* feel more positive and more creative?

A top U.S. utility assembled 20 of its training professionals for three days to redesign several of their courses with accelerated learning principles and methods. Here is the room before the design workshop (orderly but sterile) and during the workshop (untidy but stimulating). The colorful and stimulating environment proved to be relaxing and humanizing and was a big aid to everyone's creativity.

Nicky Shorey, who works at an accounting firm in London, transformed her computer training room into a south sea island. The combination of the relaxing setting and the partnering had an extremely positive impact on the learning, she says.

Details of her success are recorded in the book *The Creative Trainer* by Michael Lawlor and Peter Handley (McGraw-Hill, 1996).

Collaboration and a comfortable, happy setting helped US West Communications speed and enhance the training of customer service reps throughout its system.

Traditional classroom environments suggest:	Enhanced A.L. environments suggest:
Tension and stress	Relaxation
Boredom	Interest
Isolated individualism	Collaboration
Militarism	Humanism
Regimentation	Personal freedom
Sterility	Stimulation
Authoritarian control	Respect for people
Extrinsic motivation	Intrinsic motivation
Incarceration	Liberation
Learning is hard work	Learning is a joy

Summary of Phase 1

The goal of the Preparation Phase is to arouse learners' interest, give them positive feelings about the forthcoming learning experience, and put them into an optimal learning state. You do this through:

- positive suggestions
- learner benefit statements
- clear, meaningful goals
- creating a positive physical environment
- creating a positive emotional environment
- creating a positive social environment
- calming people's fears
- removing or reducing learning barriers
- raising questions and posing problems
- arousing curiosity and creating interest
- getting people fully involved from the start

CHAPTER 8

Phase 2: Presentation Techniques

The Presentation Phase of the learning cycle is intended to give learners an initial encounter with the learning material that initiates the learning process in a positive and engaging way.

When we hear the word "presentation," we automatically associate this with something the *facilitator* does and not with something the learners do. But we invite you in this chapter to begin to associate "presentation" with something both the facilitator and the learners do in various mixes depending on the situation. Presentation is encounter. The facilitator can lead, but the learners must do the encountering.

If you understand "presentation" as only something the facilitator does to the learner, this phase of the learning cycle becomes the weakest one by far.

Isn't it ironic? Traditional training design has put the greatest emphasis on *instructor* presentations. That's where most of the effort and money goes: *on something that has the least affect on learning.* Yet we continue to spend the bulk of our effort developing presentation materials, PowerPoint shows, teaching aids, handouts, and other consumable materials for the learner. We put, I would guess, 80% of our resources into that which has, at best, a 20% impact on the actual learning itself.

Learning, we've got to realize, comes from a learner's total, active involvement with a subject matter and not from listening to endless presentations about it. (Learning is a matter of creating knowledge, not consuming information.) Presentations exist merely to initiate the learning process and not to be the central focus of it.

> A facilitator who is always hovering over and spoon-feeding learners is a serious menace to the learning process.

The Presentation Phase of learning is not just something the facilitator does but actively involves the learner in creating knowledge every step of the way.

Idea Treasure Chest
For the Presentation Phase

What follows is a wealth of ideas of how you might get learners totally involved during:

    A. Facilitator Presentations
    B. Facilitator/Learner Presentations
    C. Learner Presentations and Discovery Exercises

A. Facilitator Presentations

Facilitator presentations are successful when they **create interest, raise curiosity,** and **jump-start the learning.** Here are a few ways you can help a presentation do this. What else can you think of?

1. Use toys, puppets, cardboard mock-ups, garage sale items, found objects, and anything else you can build or get your hands on that would add interest to your presentation and make your ideas visual and concrete.

2. When teaching a process or procedure, use craft materials to build it bigger than life on a wall, velcro board, or magnetic white board. Then have learners deconstruct and reconstruct it as a "teach-back" learning activity.

3. Tell a story with lots of human interest that illustrates the subject matter at hand.

4. Wear an appropriate costume or item of clothing while making an important point that you want learners to remember.

5. Use a sandwich board to "dress" as a computer system, a piece of technical equipment, a product, or a process. Then explain yourself to the learners in the first person as if you were that computer system or piece of equipment.

6. Use mnemonic (memory) devices to help people remember key points. (An example: "righty-tighty, lefty-loosey" helps you remember how jar covers, light bulbs, nuts and bolts, valves, and screwdrivers work.)

7. Spice your presentation with analogies and metaphors, using well-known phenomena from nature and everyday life to illustrate how the system or process or skill you are teaching works.

8. Let your presentation take the form of a talk show in which you interview a subject matter expert or experts with short, provocative questions to keep things moving.

9. Use mental imagery to help people rehearse a skill or to take an imaginary journey through a system or process.

10. Use learners as props who can wear costumes or hold keyword labels representing parts of a total process or system that you then can manipulate in front of the group to make things clear.

B. Facilitator/Learner Presentations

Since all good learning is the creation of meaning and value on the part of the learner, give learners something to create during a facilitator presentation. Here are a few ideas. What else can you think of?

1. Before a presentation, ask everyone to choose a partner. Tell everyone that they will have to create a 20-question oral exam for their partner based on the presentation they are about to experience. At the conclusion of the presentation, they will have to administer their oral examination to their partner and certify whether or not their partner has a good grasp of the learning material. Meanwhile, during the presentation, their partner will be preparing a 20-question oral exam for them.

2. Before a presentation, give each learner an index card. Ask them to print their name on it, fold it in half, and drop it into a container. Pass the container around and ask everyone to draw a card, keeping the name of the person on their card secret. Tell the people that each of them will have to prepare detailed notes on the presentation for their secret pal. (Encourage them to use color and images wherever appropriate.) After the presentation, ask people to give their notes to their secret pal while reviewing the contents with them.

3. Stop periodically in a presentation and ask small teams to discuss with each other their reactions to the information or skill just presented and how they can best apply it in their life and work.

4. Stop periodically in a presentation and have partners ask each other 5-10 questions or share what they learned and how they will apply it.

5. Before a presentation, put people in teams. Tell them that each team will have to create a 20-question quiz on the presentation for another team. At the conclusion of the presentation, give each team 10 minutes or so to create its 20-question quiz based on the questions its members have gathered during the presentation. Then have the teams exchange quizzes and answer the questions.

6. Before a presentation, give everyone a large Bingo card of 16 squares on a large sheet of paper. Randomly put in each square a term you will be explaining or a question you will be answering. Begin your presentation. As a term is explained or a question answered, the learners fill in the appropriate information on the appropriate square of their card. When a learner gets a Bingo, he or she shouts out "Bingo!", stands up, and reviews the information recorded on the card. If it is correct, the player gets a small prize and the presentation continues.

7. Put people in pairs or small teams. Give them a series of questions to answer or problems to solve based on the presentation they are about to witness. After the presentation, give them a few minutes to compare notes before sharing their results with the group.

8. Make a presentation into a press conference. Beforehand give each learner a card containing a question that they must ask the presenter. If the sequence of questions is important, number the cards. The presenter would indicate when he/she is ready for the next question.

9. Give learners one or a series of schematics or pictograms with many pieces of information missing. Ask them to see how much of the missing information they can gather and add from the presentation they are about to observe. Have them debrief their results with a partner after the presentation.

10. Give each learner a large card with a term on it that you will be explaining in your presentation. Put the definition of the term on the back of each card. As you mention the term in your presentation, the person holding that card is to jump up, display the card, and define it for the group; adding whatever additional information they can.

C. Learner Presentations and Discovery Exercises

In some cases, learners can have their initial encounter with new information or skill without a formal presentation from a facilitator. Here are a few ideas. What other ideas can you think of?

1. **Team Presentations.** Divide people into teams. Ask each team to research a subset of the subject matter at hand and make a presentation to the group. Provide teams with materials to make props and presentation aids to help them in getting their points across.

2. **Team Job Aid Creation.** Divide people into teams. Ask each team to research a subset of the subject matter at hand and to produce a one-page (or less) job aid for the whole class. Make computers and color printers available to each team if possible. Ask teams to distribute and explain their job aids to the whole class.

3. **Team Pictogram Creation.** Put people in teams. Ask each team to read a portion of the learning material and create a large, colorful mural pictogram out of it that captures the essence of what they read. Then give people time to examine each other's artwork. Or have teams explain their murals to each other.

4. **Scavenger Hunt.** Put people in teams. Give each team 20 questions to answer or 20 pieces of information to collect in a specific amount of time. Gathering some of the information could require them to leave the classroom.

5. **Investigative Interviewing.** Put people in pairs or small teams and send them into the organization to interview existing employees on some aspect of the subject matter and to report back to the group.

6. **Model Building.** Ask learners in teams or as a whole group to build a model of the process or system they are learning about. Depending on the subject and the resources available, they can build the model on the floor, on a tabletop, on a wall, or on a magnetic white board.

7. **Collaborative Pretest.** Give learners their "final exam" right at the start. Ask them to mingle and work together to see how many questions they can answer by working with each other and with the reference materials available.

8. **Problem Posing.** Pose a series of problems for learners to solve in pairs or teams relative to the subject matter at hand. Make appropriate reference materials available to them.

9. **Field Trip.** Arrange for a field trip or an "out-of-the-classroom" experience for the learners directly related to the subject matter at hand. From the experience, have them create the process, the system, or the principles underlying what they observed.

10. **Learners Create the Course.** Ask learners to create the total learning experience from scratch as if they were developing the course themselves. Have them work with the raw materials you provide to create presentations, learning exercises, job aids, learning games, peripherals, action learning scenarios, imagery exercises, final exams— everything. Then have them demonstrate their creations to each other.

Examples From the Field

What other ways are there to present new learning material other than the lecture method? What follows are some examples of what a few graduates of our *Accelerated Learning Training Methods* workshop have done to get learners totally involved.

Create Your Own Coaching Model
Major Canadian Retailer

Using the idea of "the learner as creator," Mike Adams of one of Canada's largest department store chains, shortened a coaching course for frontline managers from **two days to four hours** with great results. Ninety percent of the participants reported that their coaching skills improved significantly, as did the communication between employees and managers, and as did the measurable productivity in their departments. Here's how Mike did it.

Mike Adams

1. Right in the door, participants were given a piece of paper and asked to build an airplane.

2. They flew their airplanes in an open space from a common starting line and were then asked to stand where their plane landed.

3. They were asked to note those people whose planes flew the farthest. These were identified as the "experts."

4. People whose planes flew poorly were asked to select an expert and have this person help them build a better airplane, noting the coaching that went on.

5. The people who were coached were asked to fly their new planes. Of course, their performance improved significantly. Why? Because of the coaching, of course.

6. Next, people were put into small teams and asked to construct a coaching model based on what they just experienced— a model that could be applied to any situation.

7. Each team presented its coaching model to the class. The models were then blended into a single model that the whole class agreed on.

8. Using this model, they were then asked to practice it through a "whole class" role play (with the facilitator taking the part of the employee, and the whole class acting as the manager).

9. The class was then asked to create a job aid of the model that each manager could take back with them.

10. Next, each manager was asked to create a coaching plan (based on the model) to deal with an on-the-job situation they were currently faced with. After a team-based debriefing, the managers returned to their jobs to execute their plans.

If You Build It, They Will Sleep
If They Build It, They Will Learn
Wisconsin Electric

At Wisconsin Electric's Point Beach Nuclear Plant on Lake Michigan, the training department applied the principle that "the learning is in the doing" to a course on the electrical distribution system of the nuclear plant. Traditionally taught by lecture using overhead transparencies, it put people to sleep (including the instructors) and the learning was less than effective. Here's what they did to remedy the situation.

When learners arrived, they found the classroom totally empty of furniture, with the exception of a few tables along the walls. They were asked, as a group, to build the electrical distribution system of the plant on the floor as one giant grid. The necessary documentation for doing so was on one of the tables. All sorts of materials (poster board, markers, tape, construction paper, ribbon, etc.) were also there.

At first, learners were hesitant. This was certainly a departure from the traditional classroom they were so used to in their corporate culture. But their hesitancy vanished quickly as they organized themselves for the task. Nobody could fall asleep in this class. Everyone was active as the grid gradually took shape on the floor. And the learners did it all, the instructor functioning only as a consultant from time to time.

Once the grid was completed, the class used it as a giant visual aid as the instructor presented them with problems to solve and

"what-if" scenarios to discuss. They could even send individual learners through the grid as electrons to test their understanding of the electrical flow and what happens when outages occur. The learners loved it. One reason was that it made everything so vivid. The social nature of the experience helped too, compared with the individual isolation characteristic of most classrooms. Another reason learners loved it was because they were "hands-on" people to begin with, whose learning flourished when they could be physically active, and diminished when they were forced to be physically inactive.

The Whole Organization Is The Classroom
Major U.S. Semiconductor Manufacturer

David Andreoni was attending one of The Center for Accelerated Learning's in-house workshops at his company's huge manufacturing facility in Albuquerque. It was Friday morning, the final day of a 3-day class. The workshop had continually emphasized that *learning is best when learners are treated as creators, not consumers.*

The phone in the classroom rang. It was for David. After a brief conversation, he told us that he would have to leave the class for 90 minutes. There was a one-week orientation class for new employees going on in the next building, and this was the final day. The person who was to teach a 90-minute segment on "total safety management" that morning had called in sick at the last minute. David, who had taught the subject, was being tapped to fill in. He rushed to the next building immediately. There was no time to retrieve his teaching materials. What was he to do?

He took the plunge. Not having time to get his presentation materials together, he decided to test the idea that *the best learning is creation, not consumption.* He entered the classroom to find the new hires dazed. They had been there all week long passively sitting listening to one subject matter expert after another dump an endless stream of information on them. They were in a stupor, said David, and "dying of consumption" as we used to say.

Immediately David had them stand up. He asked them to count off in fours and divided them into four groups: the Pigs, the Dogs, the Rats, the Slugs. He then gave them their instructions. The groups were to leave the room for 20 minutes, go out into the organization, and gather information on safety by interviewing existing employees. They would then be expected to report to the class what they learned. He sent each group to a different location where they would encounter employees in transit: in front of elevators, near the parking lot, at the cafeteria exit, etc.

He instructed the groups to stop employees, explain their mission and ask them questions such as: "As new employees, what's the most important thing we should know about safety around here?"; "How can the company improve safety in the factory?"; "Where's the next accident most likely to occur?"; and "What's the greatest safety danger we face in working here?"

The learners returned lively and energetic. David asked each team to tell the group what they discovered. A lively discussion followed for 30 minutes. David said little, other than asking a few questions for clarification. The learners were totally involved and were learning from each other.

David said that everything he would have covered in a lecture was discussed, but in a much more effective way. And it had taken only 50 minutes, rather than the 90 minutes it usually took to cover the material.

The result? The learners loved it, said David.

He got a big round of applause from the group. They told him, "This was the best presentation we had all week!" David felt great. "This accelerated learning stuff really works," he told us, grinning from ear to ear.

The Trainer Creates the Context
The Learners Create the Content
Hewlett-Packard– U.K.

Lynne Watson of Hewlett-Packard in the U.K. reported that her company found a way to significantly improve its "Customer Care" program. Rather than continue to use a packaged program that treated the learners like passive consumers rather than active creators, she replaced it with a learner-centered approach that she and her associates designed in an hour and twenty minutes.

People arriving for the course immediately piled into a van and were driven to Reading, a town west of London near their training facility. They were then asked to wander around the town in pairs for an hour and a half visiting at least five businesses and observing customer service (or lack thereof) in each business. As they walked from store to store, they were asked to discuss with each other what was good in the last encounter and why, and what was not good and why, and what would they have done to make it better.

After an hour and a half of this they were driven back to the training facility where they discussed and analyzed their experiences that morning. Out of this, they developed their own principles of good customer care, printing them out immediately so everyone could have a copy. Then in teams they discussed specific ways of applying these principles in their work with their customers in the U.K.

The new course, Lynne said, was felt by everyone to be far more effective. Learners were transformed from passive consumers of someone else's ideas to active creators of their own meaning.

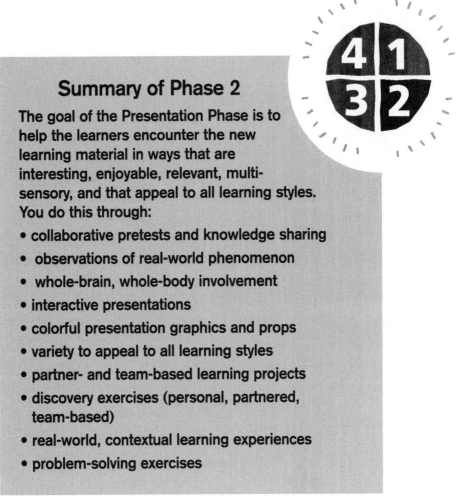

Summary of Phase 2

The goal of the Presentation Phase is to help the learners encounter the new learning material in ways that are interesting, enjoyable, relevant, multi-sensory, and that appeal to all learning styles. You do this through:

- collaborative pretests and knowledge sharing
- observations of real-world phenomenon
- whole-brain, whole-body involvement
- interactive presentations
- colorful presentation graphics and props
- variety to appeal to all learning styles
- partner- and team-based learning projects
- discovery exercises (personal, partnered, team-based)
- real-world, contextual learning experiences
- problem-solving exercises

CHAPTER 9

Phase 3: Practice Techniques

Knowledge is not something you absorb, knowledge is something you create.

Phase 3, the *practice (integration)* phase, is the very heart of accelerated learning. Without it there can be no real learning.

This phase of the learning cycle can account for 70% (or more) of a total learning experience. It's in this phase that the learning actually takes place. After all, it's what the learner thinks and says and does that creates the learning, and not what the instructor thinks, says, and does.

The Shift From Teaching to Learning

The instructor's role is simply to initiate the learning process and then get out of the way. Here's another way to put it. The instructor's task is to create a *context* in which the learner can create meaningful *content* relative to the subject matter at hand. The instructor's role is to get the learners to think, say, and do—to deal with the new learning material in ways that will help them integrate it into their existing internal structure of knowledge, meaning, and skill.

A facilitator who is always hovering over and spoon-feeding learners is a serious menace to the learning process.

It's what the learner says and does that is more important than what the facilitator says and does for the actual learning.

– Win Wenger

True Learning Changes a Person

Research into the brain and learning has revealed an astonishing fact: When something is truly learned, *the internal structure of*

a person's internal chemical/electrical nervous system is altered. Something new inside a person is created— new neural networks, new chemical/electrical pathways, new associations, new relationships. Literally. The learners must be given time for this to happen. Otherwise, nothing sticks, nothing integrates, nothing is really learned. All learning is change. Where there is no time for change, there is no real learning.

A frequent complaint about training programs is "poor retention." And this will always be the case when we do not allow time for a healthy Phase 3. That's why *hot house* learning has never worked ("Just give 'em the information."). And that's why the take-away value from so many conferences, presentations, meetings, and training programs is so low— there is no time for learners to create their own meanings, to change their internal structures, to build new neural networks and establish new habits of mind; in short— to learn.

Learner Processing

To build new structures of meaning out of experience can take many forms and is best when it involves all aspects of a person's total body/mind system.

You can think of the Presentation Phase and the Practice Phase as two sides of a tennis court. Obviously it's important for the presenter to get the ball in the learner's court as often and for as long as possible, since it's in the learner's court that the actual learning occurs. Here are some ways of doing this.

Idea Treasure Chest

For the Practice Phase

1. **Articulation.** Stop a presentation and ask people to form pairs. One person in each pair can be designated "A," the other, "B." Then have A or B explain to their partner what was just covered in the presentation as if the partner missed it all and knew nothing about it.

2. **Idea Sharing.** Stop a presentation periodically. Ask partners to talk about what they just learned. They can share the most important information or value they've gotten from the training thus far and explain to each other why it's important to them and how they plan to apply it in their professional and/or personal lives.

3. **Trial and Error.** Ask people to repeatedly go through a cycle wherein they perform a skill (even if they do it poorly at first), get immediate feedback, and perform the skill again. Ask them to talk about what they are experiencing, how they feel about it, and what they need more of to improve their performance.

4. **Collaborative Role Play.** When teaching communications, supervisory, or sales skills, have two or more people play the role of one person, with one of the members of the group acting as "the mouth." The facilitator takes the role of the other person in the dialog. Each time there is an exchange, the multiperson has 15-30 seconds to confer with itself before its "mouth" responds.

5. **Concentration.** When teaching terms and definitions, put people in pairs. Give each pair a deck of cards, half of which have terms on them, the other half of which have the matching definitions of those terms. Ask them to shuffle the deck and put the cards face down in a matrix on the table and play *Concentration*. Partners in turn pick up a card revealing a term or a definition and try to pick up the appropriate matching card. If they are unsuccessful, they return the two cards

face down to the matrix. If they are successful in finding a match, they keep the two cards. The partner with the most matching pairs "wins."

6. **Searching for Answers.** Ask learners to write down on a card three or more questions they have about a subject just covered— a term they don't understand, a concept that's fuzzy, whatever. Then ask them to get out of their seats, wander around the room, and ask each other for help in answering their questions. If one learner asks a second learner a question that the second learner can't answer, the two of them ask a third learner and even a fourth until they find the answer. They can also search through any documentation or reference materials in the room for the answer.

7. **What Did You Learn? What Are You Going to Do About It?** Ask learners to rise and to collect from as many people they can in 5 or 10 minutes the most important thing they've learned in the last period and how they plan to apply it on the job. Ask them to write their findings down on a pad or piece of paper. At the end of the exercise, ask a few people to share with the group what they discovered.

8. **Snowball Questions.** Ask everyone to write on an 8½" x 11" piece of paper a question they have about the materials just covered. Ask them to print their question so someone else can read it and to not sign their name. Then have them crush their question into a ball. Ask them to stand. Tell them there will be a 30-second snowball fight and they should see how many people they can hit with question balls. At the end of 30 seconds, stop the action and ask everyone to pick up a snowball. Tell them that they will have 3 minutes to open the snowball, read the question, and find the answer using anyone or anything in the room as a resource. Then in turn have learners read their questions and give their answers.

9. **Peer Teaching and Review.** When teaching computers or any hands-on process, put people in pairs, one partner being "A," the other "B." Ask one partner to perform a process just learned for the other as if the other never heard it before and was sight impaired, so every step in the process has to be explained out loud. Then ask partners to exchange roles.

10. **Problem-Solving Exercise.** Put people in pairs or small teams and give them a problem (or series of problems) to solve in a specified amount of time. These should be real-world problems that test their understanding of and ability to apply the knowledge and skills being learned.

11. **Card Game Review.** Give partners a deck of cards with questions on one side and answers on the other relative to the subject at hand. Ask them to shuffle the deck and put it down question-side up. Then have them take turns answering the questions. They keep the cards they answer correctly. The ones they answer incorrectly are returned to the bottom of the deck.

12. **Stump Your Buddy.** Stop a presentation periodically and ask partners to ask each other five questions about what was just presented.

13. **Musical Questions.** Give each learner a card. Ask them each to print on the card a question they have about the material just covered. While sitting at tables or standing in a large circle, play music, asking them to keep passing their question cards to the right until the music stops. When the music stops give them 3-5 minutes to research the answer to the question they are holding, using any person(s) or resources in the room to help them. Then debrief.

14. **Real-World Observations.** Where appropriate, have people in pairs leave the training room for a short period of time to observe how something they are learning about is being implemented on the job or to interview one or two existing employees regarding their experiences with it.

15. **Error Recovery.** When teaching people how to use computers or physical equipment, put learners in pairs. Have one partner put an error into the system. Ask the other partner to then recover from the error explaining what he or she learned thereby. Then reverse roles.

16. **Manipulatives.** Ask people in pairs or small teams to reconstruct a model of a system or process while talking out loud about what they are doing and explaining how everything works and interrelates. Components of the system or process could be magnetic-backed on white board, velcro-backed on fabric, flat on a tabletop or floor, or 3-dimensional on a tabletop.

17. **Acting Out a System.** Assign people roles to play in a system or process and have them act the whole thing out. This is useful for teaching things like telephone systems, order entry systems, complex processes, and the like.

18. **Art Contest.** Have learners in small teams create large pictogram murals that capture the essence of the learning material. Entries can be judged by everyone on four separate criteria: accuracy, completeness, aesthetic beauty, and creativity.

19. **Group Brain Role Play.** When teaching any skills involving a back-and-forth dialog (supervisory, sales, customer service skills, etc.), ask the whole class to stand together in one lump in the room. As a group, they are to act as the brain of a single supervisor, salesperson, or customer service rep. The facilitator acts as the counterpart in the dialog. The facilitator says something and throws a Koosh or Nerf ball into the "brain." One "neuron" catches it. But since no neuron works alone, that neuron has 30 seconds to confer with the neurons in her or his vicinity before responding and returning the ball to the facilitator. The conversation continues, stopping periodically to analyze an exchange that just took place.

20. **Materials Creation.** Have learners in teams create learning materials for each other. This could include job aids, review games, learning exercises, models to manipulate, problem-solving exercises, and so forth.

Examples From the Field

Learners Become What They're Learning
US West Cellular

US West in Seattle used a coordinated body/mind method to help new hires practice and integrate cellular telephone concepts as part of their initial training as customer service reps.

After a presentation introducing them to the terminology and concepts of cellular systems, the learners were taken outside to a patio and asked to take roles as components of a cellular system and play out various scenarios. Some took the roles of cellular phones roaming about and were given "automobile" hats to wear. Others took the roles of transmitting towers, wearing appropriate cardboard "towers" on their heads. Others assumed the roles of landline (i.e., hardwired home telephone) equipment. When calls were made, connections were established with clothesline rope between the interacting components, while the facilitator

had the learners dialog about what was going on. Learners were asked what concepts were still fuzzy for them, or what cellular transactions they would like to know more about— and then the group acted them out. After the role playing, learners in pairs were asked to summarize for each other everything they had learned about how a total cellular phone system works and how it interfaces with the hardwired, landline telephone system. Shirley Walker, Mike Patricks, and others involved in this form of "practice" were convinced that it produced far better learning than the traditional book-based study they were used to.

Learners Create Learning Vehicles
American Express

The goal of the training was to teach American Express customer service reps all the ins and outs of the OptimaCard so they could administer customer accounts accordingly. After a short presentation and the distribution of reference material, participants were asked to create a means of learning that they could share with others.

Out of craft materials provided (poster board, construction paper, markers, rubber

cement, etc.) one group created a board game that they called "Optimopoly" that helped players rehearse their understanding of all of the major concepts and procedures relative to the OptimaCard. The game was driven by decks of question cards and could be played open book to start, allowing learners to do a timed search for answers in the documentation, or it could be played with teams who could confer before giving their answers. The board game format added a dimension of fun and proved to be a stimulant to learning. The greatest learning, however, came from creating the game itself and working with others to gather and organize the information for the question/answer decks from the documentation.

Learning by Doing
The Budd Company

Barb Schuelke and Kim Voss of the Budd Company's Waupaca Foundry in Wisconsin found a way to keep the ball in the learner's court throughout a training session in machine guarding for the foundry's machine maintenance staff.

The goal was to teach the staff how to assure that all the moving parts of machines in the foundry (pulleys, belts, pinch points, etc.) were guarded properly to prevent injury to the operators.

Knowing that they were dealing with "hands-on" people, Barb and Kim abandoned the lecture method, totally

Barb and Kim display some of the imaginative machines built by their trainees.

eliminating Phase 2 of the learning cycle and going directly from Phase 1 to Phase 3. People were put into teams and given written materials and pictures of the various types of machine guards. Then with the craft materials provided, each team was asked to build a model of a machine (real or imaginative) that would illustrate machine guarding. The grand prize would go to the team that could illustrate the greatest number of different machine guards on their model.

After the teams built and explained their models to each other, it was time for Phase 4. The teams combed the factory looking for machines needing additional guarding and spent the rest of the day constructing the appropriate guarding where needed. Needless to say, the program was extremely well received and highly successful.

The president of the company was so impressed with the models that the maintenance staff had made, that he asked that they be put on display in the lobby of the main office.

Summary of Phase 3

The goal of the Practice Phase is to help learners integrate and incorporate new knowledge or skill in a variety of ways. You do this through:

- learner processing activities
- hands-on trial/feedback/reflection/retrial
- real-world simulations
- learning games
- action learning exercises
- problem-solving activities
- individual reflection and articulation
- partner- and team-based dialog
- collaborative teaching and review
- skill-building practice activities
- teachbacks

CHAPTER 10

Phase 4:
Performance Techniques

Learning is the process of turning experience into knowledge, knowledge into understanding, understanding into wisdom, and wisdom into action.

The Success Is in the Follow-Through.

The value of any learning program is revealed only in Phase 4 as the learning gets applied to the job. Yet, many training designs neglect this phase or eliminate it altogether. It's important to realize that this phase is not just an add-on, but is integral to the whole learning process. Without a strong Phase 4, the first three phases of the learning cycle can be a total waste. As any golfer or tennis player can tell you, *the success is in the follow-through.*

The Goal of the Performance Phase

The goal of the Performance Phase is to make sure the learning sticks and is applied successfully. After experiencing the first 3 phases of the learning cycle, we need to make sure that people are performing with (and continually extending) their new knowledge and skill on the job in ways that create real value for themselves, the organization, and the organization's clients. In agricultural terms, performance is in the harvest.

The Enemies of Performance

The enemies of performance and, hence, of good learning are many. Here are a few prominent ones:

Unless what is learned
is applied,
there **is** no learning.

- No immediate need to apply the knowledge or skill.
- No support system for reinforcing the learning on the job.
- A company culture or work situation antithetical to the new learning.
- No rewards for successfully applying the new knowledge or skill.
- No consequences for not applying the new knowledge or skill.
- No time to integrate and apply the new knowledge or skill.

A designer (acting as both a performance consultant and an organizational development specialist all rolled up into one) has to build a Phase 4 that removes as many of these performance barriers as possible to assure that the learning "takes" and that real value is created on the job.

The Components of Phase 4

The Performance Phase has a number of components that you can design separately and then blend. You can think of this phase as divided into two parts: 1) what learners do *at the session itself*, and 2) what they do *after the session* to apply, reinforce, and extend their learning and performance.

The success is in the
follow-through.

Performance Phase Components

I. At the Session:
  A. Dress rehearsal
  B. Evaluating the learning
  C. Evaluating (& enhancing) the learning program
  D. Planning on-the-job applications

II. After the Session:
  A. Reinforcing the learning
  B. Assuring organizational support for the new learning
  C. Evaluating on-the-job performance
  D. Enhancing the performance

Idea Treasure Chest

For the Performance Phase

Here are some ideas for each of the components of the Performance Phase.

I. At the Session

A. Dress Rehearsal

Have learners "put it all together" and, through *job-performance simulations*, perform with the new learning as they would on the job. It's important to make the *job-performance simulation* as real-world and contextual as you possibly can. Here are a few ideas:

1. **Task Performance.** Ask learners to perform an entire job task from start to finish while they describe out loud what they're doing. If it's, let's say, a course on doing computerized billing, have people process actual bills and check each other's work. If it's a course on WordPerfect, ask people to use the software to do a portion of their daily work in class.

2. **Role Play.** Ask learners to role-play how they might deal with real situations on the job as supervisors, managers, customer service reps, or whatever roles they're preparing for. If individual role plays would create too much stress for people, have them do *collaborative* role plays where 2 or 3 people take the role of one person, allowing them 15-30 seconds to confer with each other before one of them, acting as the mouth, responds.

3. **Real-World Problem Solving.** Pose real problems (relative to the subject matter) that need to be solved in the organization. Ask people to apply what they've learned to these problems in ways that can be immediately implemented.

4. **Partnered Performance Rehearsal.** Put people in pairs. Give each pair a deck of cards containing complex, real-world situations that they are likely to encounter on the job. In turn, have each partner pick a card, read it, and describe in detail how they would handle the situation based on what they learned in the class. Ask the "listening" partner to ask questions and offer a critique of their partner's approach, emphasizing what was done well and making suggestions, where possible, as to how to make it better.

B. Evaluating the Learning

It's important to know to what extent the learning program has been successful. One way, which is by no means the only way or the best way, is to give people tests (before and after), problem-solving exercises, oral examinations, hands-on demonstrations of competency, or whatever would lend itself to the subject matter at hand. Some ideas:

1. **Pretest & Posttest.** Test people's knowledge of a subject before and after the learning program to measure gain. If you're interested not so much in individual gain as in the aggregate gain of the group as a whole, let the pretest and posttest be done by everyone anonymously.

2. **Show-You-Know Exercise.** Ask people to show their competency by performing a process or series of processes central to the learning while they talk out loud about what they're doing and why.

3. **Oral Examination.** To test people's understanding, have them answer a series of questions out loud, solve a series of problems, or describe in an open-ended way everything they have learned about the subject at hand.

4. **Learners Cross-Test Each Other.** Put people in pairs. Ask each partner to prepare a 20-30–question examination for their counterpart. Then have partners administer their tests to each other, checking the results and critiquing each other's performance. The examinations can be oral, written, or a combination of both. In some cases, you can have teams instead of individuals do this exercise.

C. Evaluating (and Enhancing) the Learning Program

No training program should ever be set in cement. Rather, it should be constantly evolving and improving throughout its life. Learners can help you do this in a number of ways. For example:

1. **Team-Based Evaluation.** Put learners into teams and give each team several minutes to critique the learning program, coming up with three to five ways of making it better. Have them record their ideas on a flipchart or overhead transparency and report out loud to the whole group.

2. **Class-Based Evaluation.** Tell learners that you want them to critique the learning program together while you are out of the room. Ask them to appoint a scribe and record on one flipchart learners' responses to the question "What went well?" and on another "What might make it better?" Leave the room for five or ten minutes. When you return, debrief the flipcharts with the group.

3. **Individual-Based Evaluation.** Give each learner several index cards at the start of a program. Immediately after each lesson or portion of the training ask them to record on the cards their reaction— what they liked about it and how they think it could be improved. Collect the cards throughout the program.

4. **Ball-Toss Evaluation.** Have learners form a circle and toss a ball around to each other for a few minutes. Ask the person catching the ball to state one thing they liked about the training program before tossing the ball to someone else. Do the exercise a second time, asking people to offer ideas for enhancing the learning program. Record this session on a tape recorder, camcorder, or flipchart.

5. **Person-on-the-Street Interviews.** Give a tape recorder or camcorder to a couple of participants and ask them to do periodic, fast-paced interviews of their classmates during breaks, asking them what they are finding most valuable in the training and soliciting any ideas they might have for improving the learning experience. Study the tape(s) after the class, implementing all the suggested enhancements that you can.

D. Planning On-the-Job Applications

In terms of *real learning,* only what is immediately applied to the job sticks. To help with this transference of value from the learning program to the job, ask learners to plan their applications during class. This can take a number of forms:

1. **Planning Structural Changes.** If appropriate to the subject matter, ask people to draw up detailed plans of how they will restructure their workplace or their part of the organization to accommodate and support the new learning.

2. **Planning Personal Implementations.** In classes on such subjects as coaching or supervisory skills, ask people to come up with detailed plans for using what they learned in the class to improve the productivity of specific people who report to them. Ask them to have a team of their peers discuss, enhance, and sign off on their plans. Then a few weeks later, have the same teams review each other's implementation.

3. **Planning Process Improvements.** Where appropriate, ask people to apply their new learning to improving a process under their responsibility. Have them share their plans with a team for enhancement, and debrief the outcomes with their teams later on after their plans have been implemented.

4. **Creating Job Aids.** Ask learners, individually or in teams, to create job aids that they can use to reinforce their learning and enhance their performance once they are back at work.

II. After the Session

A. Reinforcing the Learning

Since the success is in the follow-through, reinforcement of the learning in the workplace is paramount. One study discovered that without immediate application and support on the job, only 5% of classroom learning stuck. But with immediate application and proper coaching and support, 90% of the learning survived. Here are some things you can do to make sure that learning sticks:

1. **Team-Based Support Group.** Have learners get together periodically after the training for mutual consulting regarding implementing the new learning on the job. They can share their successes as well as their frustrations and challenges as they help each other apply the new learning more effectively in their day-to-day situations at work.

2. **On-Going Mentoring.** Assign mentors to new graduates of a training program who will coach the graduates for a specific amount of time in order to reinforce

and extend their learning on the job. Mentors can be earlier graduates of the same training program who themselves have been mentored and who have gained job experience with the new learning.

3. **Workplace Reminders.** You can surround graduates with a varied stream of reminders that can help them reinforce and extend their learning on the job over time. You can put tips and reminders on e-mail, on snack machines, next to water coolers, in elevators, above clocks, on bulletin boards, on lunch room tables, on "Take One" tip-of-the-week cards, on rest room mirrors, next to coffee servers, on job aids, on mobiles and wall peripherals in the office, etc., etc.

4. **MultiMedia Reinforcers.** Send graduates periodic short audiotapes filled with tips, reminders, and interviews with people who are applying the new learning successfully. Or you can create and circulate short, camcorded videos containing testimonials, examples, tips, and reminders. Play the videos on a loop where people take their breaks.

B. Assuring Organizational Support

Often new learning evaporates because there is no reward for applying it and no consequence for not, or because the organization culture or its systems are resistant to the new learning. It is the designer's role, then, to identify those organizational blocks to learning that exist and to work with others on many levels of the organization to remove or reduce them.

1. **Learning Implementation Team.** Form a team of people from multiple levels in the organization to do a performance audit and to identify and analyze any organizational blocks to the new learning that may exist. The team can then generate concrete plans and proposals for removing those blocks, getting around them, or reducing their impact. They can suggest positive ways that the organization can modify its systems and processes (or create new ones) to help reinforce the application of the new learning on the job.

2. **Reward Systems.** Recognize and compensate people on the basis of how well they are applying the new learning to the job and creating the anticipated value.

3. **Management Support.** Train managers in how to support and reinforce the new learning in their people. Recognize and reward the managers accordingly.

4. **Learner Implementation.** In collaboration with managers, assign specific job-related tasks to graduates that would require them to apply the new learning to some important aspect of the organization's work within a specified time frame.

C. Evaluating On-the-Job Performance

It's important to calculate, as much as you can, how the training is enhancing job performance and what value is being brought to the organization as a result. Here are some ways of doing this:

1. **Criterion-Referenced Evaluation.** Determine 1) what constitutes good performance, and 2) what desired *end values* should be produced for the organization and its customers as a result. (Examples of end values are things like a 10% increase in sales, a 25% reduction in customer dissatisfaction, etc.) Then let managers evaluate their people on the basis of each of the criteria established. Publish the results.

2. **Open-Ended Interviews.** Interview managers and supervisors to get their feelings regarding the job performance of the people who report to them. Ask them to tell you how and why these people are better, the same, or worse than people previously trained for the job.

3. **Learner Self-Evaluation.** Ask graduates to report on what they did to apply the new learning to the job, what difference it made for them, and what value it produced for the organization. Keep these reports in an intranet file and share them with all graduates of the training program.

D. Enhancing the Performance

People need to keep on learning and improving their knowledge, skill, and value-producing abilities throughout their lives. Since the best kind of learning comes from doing the work itself, it's important to make the whole organization a classroom where people can continually learn from everyone and everything. Here are a few ideas of what you might do to provide for this:

1. **Suggestions From Graduates.** Interview a cross section of graduates. Ask them questions like, "Now that you're back at work, what do you need more of to help you do your job better?" or "What additional knowledge or skills do you wish

you had to make you more successful at what you do?" If patterns emerge, provide people with appropriate job aids, coaching, and continuing educational experiences.

2. **Suggestions From Managers.** Interview managers of the graduates and ask them questions such as, "What additional knowledge and skills do your people need to make them more successful in their jobs?" Provide the graduates with job aids, coaching, and continuing educational experiences in those areas most often cited.

3. **The Buddy System.** Provide a framework where on-the-job partners can take responsibility for each other's continual learning and performance improvement. You can arrange for people to change learning partners periodically as appropriate.

4. **Team-Based Learning.** Get graduates together at regular intervals to exchange experiences, review their progress, and help each other bolster their knowledge and skill in areas of their greatest need. Adopt a policy of *learners teaching learners* wherever possible.

Examples From the Field

Accelerated Learning Resource Center
Ontario Hydro - Canada

Larry Barnett of Ontario Hydro established an in-house resource center he calls *Accelerated Learning Alley* to serve the on-going learning needs of trainers in his organization. It's an open area surrounded by trainers' cubicles in the middle of his organization's training center. There's a round table where trainers can read and meet with one another to exchange ideas.

A bookcase is loaded with resources: books and magazines, A.L. Newsletters, visual course maps, and samples of colorful classroom materials created by instructors.

Balloons and a colorful *Accelerated Learning Alley* sign hangs from the ceiling. To further support on-going learning and continual performance improvement, Larry arranges for the instructors to meet periodically in a special room for lunch to share the successes they've been having with accelerated learning and to brainstorm new ideas.

Action Plan Reinforcement
Sharon Bowman

As part of the Performance Phase of her job skills program for dislocated workers, consultant Sharon Bowman gives each participant a 3x5 index card. On the front they write their name and their phone number. On the back they write the first stage of their action plan that they are going to implement immediately after the workshop.

Sharon Bowman

She asks participants to form standing pairs and share their action plans with each other. At a signal, they exchange cards and find a new partner. They read the action plans from the cards they are now holding and exchange cards again. At a signal they perform this process a third time. After the third exchange, people are asked to put the card they are holding in a safe place and take it with them after the workshop. They are asked to call that person whose card they are holding at the end of one week to find out how their action plan is going and to offer any council and encouragement they can.

Follow-Through Monthly Updates
Training Partner - London

David Gibson of *Training Partners* in the U.K. teaches Office97 to clients all over Europe. As an extra service and to assure that learners keep learning after their initial training, David provides his 2700 graduates with a monthly publication filled with tips, shortcuts, tricks, and quick reviews of how to use the various features of the software. Much of the content of the publication is driven by the Help Desk calls that David receives from the field as part of his support services — so he knows his publication is meeting real needs.

For additional support after the initial training, learners can sign up for an hour's session with a facilitator at any time, and for as many times as they wish, to review any aspect(s) of the software that may still be confusing to them.

Follow-Through Support Meetings
Toronto Accelerated Learning League

Graduates of the *Accelerated Learning Training Methods Workshop* from the greater Toronto area have formed a follow-through consortium called TALL (Toronto Accelerated Learning League). Members from American Express, Zurich Canada, Canadian Tire, Bank of Montreal, Masterpiece Corporation, The Training Oasis and other Canadian organizations meet periodically for on-going reinforcement, idea exchange, and support in implementing accelerated learning methods in their organizations. Though they started small, as you can see in the picture at the left, their last half-day meeting attracted 50 people. Member organizations provide free space and refreshments to the group to encourage the follow-through effort.

Follow-Through Learning Fair
CIGNA Group Insurance

Diane Unger, Director of Organization Learning at CIGNA Insurance and a strong proponent of A.L., organized a Learning Fair to reinforce the use of accelerated learning methods throughout her organization. At the fair, A.L. practitioners exhibited their materials and designs and shared their successes with those newly trained in the A.L. approach. Here, Andy Kantner, Assistant Director of Human Resources models a giant poncho that his team made to review some of the major aspects of A.L.

The Fair helped strengthen everyone's dedication to this new and more effective approach to learning, says Diane.

Summary of Phase 4

The goal of the Performance Phase is to help learners apply and extend their new knowledge or skill to the job so that the learning sticks and performance continually improves. You do this through:

- immediate real-world application
- creating and executing action plans
- follow-through reinforcement activities
- post-session reinforcement materials
- on-going coaching
- performance evaluation and feedback
- peer support activities
- supportive organizational and environmental changes

PART 4

Additional A.L. Tools and Techniques

CHAPTER 11

Music for Learning

Throughout human history, music has always been an integral part of life. Significant events in all ancient civilizations were often accompanied by singing and chanting or by someone beating on something, strumming on something, or blowing on something. From weddings, to rites of passage, to funerals, to celebrations, to religious rituals, to educational events of all kinds, music was always there.

Western industrial culture, however, with its tendency to compartmentalize everything, has disconnected music from learning. We still use music as an aid to children's learning, but when it comes to adults, learning is centered on words alone. Music, rhythm, and bodily movement have been banished as aids to learning. That's unfortunate, because music and learning belong together. The reason is physiological.

Music and Memory

The Lymbic System of the human brain (see Chapter 4 on *The Brain and Learning*) contains equipment involved in processing music. The same Lymbic System contains equipment essential for long-term memory. Music and memory are physiologically connected in the brain.

This would explain why a high school student who finds it impossible to memorize the Periodic Table of Elements in chemistry class knows perfectly the lyrics of 150 different songs— without even trying. Music and memory are linked in the brain.

The Brahman priests of India used rhythm and music to memorize volumes of Vedic texts. The *Iliad* and *Odyssey* of Homer were poems (raps really) often recited out loud to

background rhythm and music. Children today learn their ABC's through music and their multiplication tables through rhythmic patter. And advertisers use music and rhythm all the time to put their messages inside of us.

The Bulgarian educator and researcher, Georgi Lozanov, developed a method for accelerating language training through suggestion, relaxation, and the use of music. And at the University of California in Irvine, researchers found that students who listened to Mozart music prior to testing their ability to process spatial information scored 8 and 9 points higher than those who listened to a recorded *verbal* relaxation message instead.

It's obvious that all of us in education and training need to re-discover the many positive contributions music can make to learning.

The Benefits of Music

Music need not always be present for learning to occur, of course, but it can enhance learning in a number of ways. You can use music to:

- Warm, humanize, and energize the learning environment.
- Relax and open the mind for learning.
- Create positive feelings and associations in the learner.
- Create "upshifting" in the brain.
- Promote multisensory learning.
- Aid in accelerating and enhancing the learning process.

Music affects feelings. And feelings affect learning. The right kind of music tends to have both a relaxing and stimulating effect on the brain and on the whole nervous system. Music properly used, then, can help people bring more of their total capabilities into play as they engage the power of their full minds for learning.

One caution: resist the temptation to become dogmatic and exclusive about the type of music you use. There is no standard *right* music for the classroom. The music that is right is the music that contributes to relaxation, alertness, openness, and optimal learning for a particular audience.

The Uses of Music for Classroom Learning

Here are just a few ways music can be used as an adjunct to learning.

- **Prelude to Learning**
  Playing music while people arrive for a learning event can have a welcoming effect, warming the environment, creating interest, and calming the mind.

- **Breaks**
  Music during breaks helps maintain a pleasant learning environment, keeping people both relaxed and energized.

- **Mental Imagery Scenarios**
  If you use mental imagery for problem solving, skill rehearsal, idea generation, or attitude setting, special meditative music can help create the mood.

- **Concert Preview**
  Material to be learned can be previewed to the accompaniment of music.

- **Concert Review**
  You can use music to accompany reviews of learning material via overheads, slides, posters, or computer-generated shows.

- **Presentations**
  Music can be used in the background during stories, dramatic readings, demonstrations, or presentations by slides, overheads, video, or computer.

- **Learning Exercises**
  Appropriate background music can be used during various individual, partnered, or group learning exercises (tests, problem solving, idea generation, model building, quiet study, peer tutoring, group dialog, learning games, etc.).

- **Songs & Raps**
  These can be provided by the designer or facilitator or created by the learners themselves as a method for remembering key ideas, terms, concepts, and processes and for celebrating learning.

- **Themes**
  If a learning program has a theme, theme-related music can be used to set the mood and complement the learning.

- **Postlude**
  Appropriate "exit music" can create a friendly and energizing environment for concluding a program and exchanging farewells.

The Uses of Music for Self-Paced Learning

Audiocassettes, videotapes, and multimedia programs can all be enhanced with the addition of appropriate music. Music can be used in the background during the presentation of new material and for concert previews and reviews.

Music on audiocassette or CD can be provided as a study aid to calm and focus the mind during personal study periods. This will not appeal to everyone (Some people can't study when there is music in the environment.), but it will appeal to many.

You can provide presentations, concert reviews, museum tours, and mental imagery scenarios on audiotapes (with music backgrounds) that people can use to reinforce their learning inside and outside of the classroom.

What Kind of Music Is Best?

The best kind of music is that which improves learning effectiveness. Period. This can vary from culture to culture and from audience to audience. Accelerated learning practitioners in the West tended until recently to emphasize the use of classical baroque music for learning— since it was this type of music that Georgi Lozanov used in his research on accelerating language training in the 1970's.

Baroque music and other classical music are fine choices for many situations and many audiences. The right high-quality "New Age" music can also work for many situations too. So can jazz. And so can all sorts of music from non-Western cultures. It is important not to become dogmatic about the type of music you use. Experiment, exercise discretion, and use what works.

It's often best to have a variety of music. Slow pieces can set a tranquil mood. Jazz can set a bright, peppy mood. Sousa marches or African drums or South American rhythmic dance music can set a mood of high energy. It can all work, and all work together.

Whatever music you choose, it should have a degree of depth and spirit and soul to it. Elevator music and some forms of popular music are often too shallow to have an enriching affect on the human mind and spirit.

Caveat

To assure that you are not violating copyright by your use of music in the classroom, you can secure permission from the publisher to use it. You may be able to get some direction on this by calling the American Society of Composers, Authors, and Publishers (ASCAP) in New York City at 212-621-6000.

Royalty-Free Music

Some royalty-free music advertised for education is really of very low quality and should be avoided. It is simply too shallow to speak to the full personality. One organization that offers a variety of high-quality royalty-free music is *LifeSounds*. Call them at 1-888-687-4251 and ask for their free catalog.

Some Suggestions

Check the Resources section of this book for additional suggestions on music for learning.

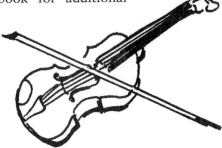

CHAPTER 12

Themes

Course themes can, in many cases, be a valuable aid to learning. Many people have found that the right theme for the right audience and the right subject matter can be a big help in promoting better and faster learning. But themes have to be used with discretion. A theme inappropriately used can be counterproductive and a big waste of time. Themes work best when they fit the occasion and are directly or metaphorically related to the course content.

A theme can aid the learning process when it:

- helps tie the subject matter together.
- creates an atmosphere of fun.
- relaxes and energizes the learners.
- inspires everyone's creativity.
- humanizes the learning process.
- helps generate ideas for learning activities.
- provides ideas for dressing up the environment.

Types of Themes

The possibilities are endless. Training professionals have used a wide range of themes successfully. Here's a short sampling.

Journey: Cruise
Train trip
Plane trip
Hiking trip
Space journey

Sports: Baseball
Basketball
Football
Car racing
Olympics
Mountain climbing

Literature:
Jack and the Beanstalk
Alice in Wonderland
The Wizard of Oz
Sherlock Holmes
Dr. Seuss
Treasure Island

Recreation:
Summer camp
Hawaiian luau
Mexican fiesta
A day at the beach
Camping

Entertainment:
Movie
Game show
Circus or fair
TV show
Theater production

Miscellaneous:
Restaurant
Jungle survival
Hospital
Picnic
Gardening
Mystery

Getting the Most Out of Themes

Never let a theme take on so much importance that it eclipses the main aim of the learning itself. If a theme helps you achieve better end results, use it. If not, don't. Themes, like all learning techniques, are not ends in themselves. But they can be useful in so far as they foster better, happier learning and improved job performance.

Multiple themes can be used for longer courses (such as weeks-long initial training for customer service reps). Changing themes periodically can keep everyone's interest up. And the learners themselves can help enhance and embellish each new theme with their ideas.

Themes can sometimes be suggested by the content itself. Seven topics suggest a theme of sailing to the seven seas. Nine topics can suggest a nine-hole golf course. Four topics can suggest the four quarters of a basketball game.

Examples From the Field

To start you thinking about what you might do, here are several examples of what people have already done— all successful applications of themes.

Hospital Theme
American Express

To help customer service reps learn how to "cure" customer dissatisfaction, Lynn Simek and others at the American Express call center in Greensboro, NC, used a hospital theme. They named the course *Curing an Ailing Card Member.* Prior to the class, each participant was sent a toy doctors' kit containing a stethoscope, syringe, tongue depressor, bandage, gauze, and other medical paraphernalia, each labeled with a statement that related the item to course objectives.

Arriving at class, learners walked into an environment decorated like an emergency room. Music from *MASH* was playing. There was a big red cross on the wall. The two facilitators were dressed in white medical coats and stethoscopes. On a table in the middle of the room was a manikin (the ailing customer) all bandaged up. The bandages were labeled with the various ailments that customers could suffer. People were placed in diagnostic teams, each team given one of these ailments to "cure."

Teams had to diagnose the reasons behind the ailment they had been given, create strategies and prescriptions for cure, and present their findings to the group together with a job aid summary that people could use at their desks to remind them of how to handle this ailment the next time they encountered it on the job.

Using this theme allowed Lynn and her associates to design the learning intervention quickly. It took them only an hour and a half to put it all together, and it assured that learners would have a high level of involvement and, hence, a successful learning experience.

The Wizard of Oz
Hewlett-Packard - The U.K.

Lynne Watson used the theme of *The Wizard of Oz* to enhance a course on career development for H-P employees in England. Classroom decorations and Oz music set the scene. As an initial exercise, people worked with partners to give the Tin Man within  them a heart by answering the question: "What is your heart telling you that you should be doing with your life?"

Once each person had worked through that question and gotten clarity on what they should be doing with their lives, they next had to exercise their brains (the Scarecrow) to figure out a career plan based on what their heart was telling them.

Once they had their plan in place, they had to have the courage to put it into effect (enter the Lion). Along the way, people could identify the flying monkeys and wicked witches in their lives that put obstacles in their way and identify their good helpers who could assist them in overcoming those obstacles.

Here again is a case where a theme provided a context in which learners could work with each other to create their own unique content.

Baseball Theme
GM - Allison Transmission

In the newly reengineered work environment of GM's Allison Transmission/ UAW Local 933, shop floor workers are now required to operate a number of machines instead of just one — and for this they need extra training.

The problem is that most training has been tedious and unpopular with shop workers who are used to active physical movement and hate sitting in classrooms for long periods. With this in mind, Jeff Robinette and Stan Molesky used a baseball theme to

get people active and involved in a class on machine grinding. As a class announcement, participants get a ticket to a baseball game with all the pertinent information printed on it (i.e., date, time, place).

When participants arrive at the oversize room, the song "Take Me Out to the Ballgame" is playing on the boom box. There is a velvet baseball diamond on the wall at the front of the room with velcro-backed pieces bearing team names. Half of the room has been cleared of tables, and big

The batting keeps people motivated. They pay a lot more attention because they're having fun. – Jeff Robinette

signs like "Out," "Home Run," and "Double" decorate a side wall. In one corner of the room, a lab is set up with grinding wheels and a grinding instrument, called a profilometer, that they will learn to use.

After learners take a preinventory of their current knowledge, Jeff puts people in pairs, asking each pair to choose a baseball team name for themselves.

The learners then study short, 15-minute sections of the technical information followed by a 20-minute interactive class discussion. After each round of study and discussion, learners in partnered teams have to answer a series of questions. If they answer them correctly they earn a round of batting.

To bat, one partner stands up to the plate and the other partner pitches a nerf baseball. The batter gets three chances to get a hit,

determined by what sign on the wall the ball hits. If it hits the wall but not one of the signs, the batter earns a single. After they bat, they move their playing piece to the appropriate place on the wall diamond where it stays until the next time they bat.

"The batting keeps people motivated," says Jeff. "They want to get through the next round of study so they can bat again. It adds energy. And they pay a lot more attention because they're having fun."

The afternoon starts with a demonstration of the profilometer and an hour-long lab where each partnered team gets a chance to use the equipment. A round of batting follows. Then the class plays a question-and-answer game. Jeff poses a question and the learners use buzzers with lights attached for competing for the chance to answer it. The first team to buzz has 15 seconds to answer the question and cite where the answer is to be found in the documentation. (This gives them practice in using the reference manual— something that will help them back on the job.) Each correct answer earns one batting round.

The class has been so popular, says Jeff, that people are calling up asking to take it before their managers have determined if they need it — an unprecedented phenomenon in the history of the company. In Jeff's words, "It's the baseball game that brings energy to the class and therefore dramatically improves the learning process."

Camping Theme
3M Logistics

3M's Logistics Division performs many roles within 3M: distribution, customer service, order processing, and more. To help both new and experienced employees better understand these rules and improve their work processes, Cindy Macechko, Tammy Torbert, and Pam Dixon designed a one-day class around a camping theme.

To get participants primed prior to the program they are asked to go "canoeing on-line" on the Logistics home page and answer a series of questions from information they find there.

When learners arrive for class, they are welcomed to Camp Logistics by a camp counselor. Rocks and logs in the middle of the room simulate a campfire. Course content is displayed on the walls in huge peripherals. As an icebreaker, learners are given a list of acronyms specific to Logistics and are asked to work together to identify them using each other's knowledge as well as information implanted in the wall peripherals.

Next is the flag raising ceremony in which people are reminded of the vision, values, and goals of the organization and shown, in picture form, the main objectives of the day's session. Then the group gathers around the campfire to hear a "trailblazing story" by a Logistics pioneer recounting the history of the division and urging everyone to keep the pioneering spirit alive.

Camp counselors then divide the participants into cabin groups. Each group is given a

backpack of course materials which they inventory as they get to know each other. Next, the cabin groups review their answers to the "canoeing on-line" they did before class and win "Knowledge Tokens" for each correct answer which they can redeem for snacks and prizes at the Camp PX.

What would a camp be without field games? So the cabin teams participate in various games and exercises to sharpen their skills at improving the processes under their jurisdiction.

At noon, it's picnic time, and the campers enjoy a "Lunch with Leaders." The division's major leaders come to lunch and each one sits with one of the cabin groups for questions and open discussion about any aspect of the division's business.

After lunch everyone returns with the leaders to the campfire area where, laid out on the floor, is a giant display of all the components of the division's Customer Order Fulfillment

Process. The campers are invited to ask the leaders questions about the process, and discussion follows.

A rainstorm then ensues. Thunder claps play on the boom box and counselors don raincoats as they lead the group "inside" for a Rainy Day Activity, which is — how to better serve their internal customers. The counselers do some role-play demonstrations and then divide the group into two teams for further role plays.

The final activity of the day is "The Pioneer Paradigm Wagon Trip." The counselors post a huge map of the United States on the wall on which are marked all the 31 Logistics locations throughout the country. Cabin groups have to visit all 31 sites while answering 31 questions one at a time, using each other, their materials, and the wall

peripherals as resources. Each correct answer wins a certain number of miles which allows them to advance to another location and answer another question. At the end of this exercise, the questions are reviewed and the cabin groups get Knowledge Tokens for the questions they answered correctly.

The class ends with the closing ceremony — the lowering of the flag. The campers use their tokens to shop for small prizes at the camp store and, after completing their evaluations of the training, a camp photo is taken.

Cindy says that the results have been "phenomenal." She is "extremely impressed and gratified with how much the learners are walking away with."

The Great Train Robbery
MetLife

A train robbery that includes a shootout set the stage for polishing the skills of MetLife disability insurance underwriters during a five-day training program put together by Regina Libby and her team. The program had been characterized by team members as "snoozer training," but the team changed all that.

Using a train theme, learners received an invitation to a free train trip to Chicago on the Met DisAbility Train Line. The invitation contained an itinerary (program topics), trip highlights (a summary of course content), and an introduction to the train staff (the facilitators).

The training room in Chicago was decorated with a huge poster of a train and other peripherals related to the theme. Toy trains were centerpieces on the tables. As participants entered the room they were greeted by train music and welcomed by the facilitators dressed as conductors. Teams of 5 or 6 sat at tables named after well-known trains.

The learners were given a "Benefits Menu" as they reviewed the 35 major benefits of MetLife's disability policies, each benefit associated with a special icon. A PowerPoint presentation of the icons followed in which learners had to identify the benefit

associated with each icon. "This worked extremely well," said Regina.

Then just as the lunch break was being announced, a train robber (Barbara Bach) burst into the room on her fake horse with her popgun blazing yelling, "Reach for the Sky!" The surprised passengers, amused by it all, raised their arms as the robber stole something from each table. Then the sheriff (Lisa Hornsberger) entered the room and a shoot-out ensued, ending with the wounded robber lying on the floor. The sheriff assured the passengers that they were safe now and that they would discuss the experience and settle all claims after lunch.

Back from lunch, each table group was given an envelope containing information about one of the passengers on the train who was injured in some way (physically or emotionally) by the events of the robbery and had subsequently filed a disability claim. Teams had to use what they had learned in the morning to decide whether to accept or deny the claim. Then each team presented their decision to the whole group, justifying why and how they had arrived at

their decision.

Occasionally throughout the day, the passengers would go to the lounge car for entertainment where a Jeopardy game, hosted by one of the facilitators in a sequined jacket, would review people's understanding of the subject matter. All passengers played and were rewarded with play money for correct answers which they could use to purchase prizes at the end of the day.

Passengers were challenged throughout the day to write lyrics to the song "Choo Choo Charlie Was an Engineer" that reflected the subject matter of the course. The best entry won a prize at the end of the day.

The training was deemed excellent by all measures. Here's a case where a theme made a valuable contribution. Says Valerie Beilfuss, "The whole thing just came together so beautifully. It was one of the most fun and effective experiences I have ever had as a trainer."

The MetLife Team

- Regina Libby
- Barbara Bach
- Valerie Beilfuss
- Denise Fullerton
- Lisa Hornsberger
- Charles Houston

Detective Theme
Zurich Canada

Verity Seldon Dimock faced a challenge at Zurich Insurance of Canada. She had 4 1/2 days to teach dry, technical insurance information to inexperienced new hires preparing to be insurance telemarketers. They had to pass a licensing exam as the condition for their continuing employment.

To ease some of the trainees' anxiety, she hit upon using a Detective theme, calling the course "Taking the Mystery out of Insurance."

Before the class, learners get an invitation to attend the reading of the last will and testament of a Colonel Desmond Burgess, an insurance executive who has possibly been murdered. The training room is decorated to represent the library in the Colonel's home with the lights turned low and candles set around. Propped in front of the computers around the perimeter of the room are large colored prints mounted on cardboard— the Colonel's art collection.

Learners sit at tables in the middle of the room while Verity, the executor, reads the will. They learn that the Colonel has two sons, Roger and Ridley, who disappointed the Colonel by not following him into the insurance business. Now, the only way they can collect on the will is, with the

help of the class, to learn enough about insurance to pass the licensing exam in 4 1/2 days.

Verity hands everyone a card with either a question or an answer on it regarding the subject matter of the class. Learners find their matching partner, discuss their question/answer, and present this information to the class.

Lecture is kept to a minimum as learners work individually, in pairs, and in teams completing case studies, preparing presentations, and handling a number of hypothetical claims.

Teams then have to make underwriting decisions regarding a number of scenarios that are presented to them, justifying their decisions on the basis of what they just learned. Only 4 hours into the course and learners are making decisions about insurance coverages and claims, doing what actual underwriters do in their jobs.

Next, learners are given two index cards containing information on two different auto accident claims. They have to process these claims by posting their cards in one of four categories on a huge grid in the front of the room (Collision, Comprehensive, All Risks, Claim Denied) while they explain the reason for their decision to process the claim in that way. A discussion follows.

Verity then hands each learner a list of fill-in-the-blank questions to answer. They have to use their best detective skills to find the answers hidden in wall peripherals posted around the room. Other active, discovery-type exercises fill the 4 1/2 days.

Navigating in a Sea of Change
Creative Training Company

A team of trainers in Carol Hewer's A.L. Training Skills Workshop in England were asked to create an action learning exercise that would help people learn how to manage change.

The team decided on the theme of Navigating the Turbulent Sea of Change, because facing change is like paddling a boat through shark- and mine-infested waters to a distant island that keeps changing its position the closer you get to it.

They upturned a table and made it into a boat, and they made paper hats and paddles for the crew. A potted tree with an inflated parrot on it became the island. As the crew moved toward the island, other learners took the roles of mines bobbing up and down in the sea and holding signs depicting various barriers they face in bringing about positive change. When a boat hits a mine, the crew has to discuss ways of overcoming that particular barrier. If the "mine" agrees with the crew's solutions, the boat proceeds. Otherwise it sinks.

The crew also has to dialog with the instructor dressed as "Harry the Hammerhead Shark" who draws more ideas out of

The Result? The theme and all the active exercises worked together to bring the level of anxiety down and the level of learning up.

the crew as to how to navigate through the sea of change.

Only when they overcome the barriers and gather sufficient navigational strategies do they reach the "Island of Accepted Change." When they do, they receive a treasure chest filled with gold-covered chocolate coins.

"It was great fun," says Carol, "and the understanding of issues related to managing change has stayed vividly with this group since the session."

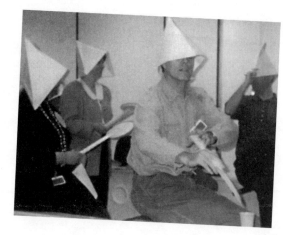

CHAPTER 13

Pictograms

Throughout recorded history, picture language was used extensively for human communication. With few exceptions, all ancient civilizations used and valued icons, symbols, and images.

However, the invention of the printing press in the 1440s changed all that. Pictures and images were difficult and time-consuming to produce on that first printing press. Words were easy. And so in the West, words were thus elevated over images as the standard for communication and education. Where alphabet literacy increased, the use of images decreased.

The turn toward words and away from images supported a left-brain emphasis in Western culture, since the left brain is dominant in the processing of words, and the right brain is dominant in the processing of images. Today, however, as we strive for a whole-brain approach to life and learning, both words and images are needed. Hence Pictograms. Pictograms simply combine images with words in endless variety.

Accelerated Learning, which emphasizes whole-brain, whole-body processing, encourages the use of pictograms of all kinds in a variety of forms for speeding and enhancing learning and human information processing.

The Uses of Pictograms

To start you thinking, here are a few ideas for the use of pictograms in education and training.

Curriculum Design

Pictograms can be helpful aids in curriculum design and course development. They can help a designer get ideas down quickly and see their relationships. And the color and pictures and relaxed fun can help make the design process more creative and more stimulating.

Words alone can retard the design process. Words and images used together can accelerate it. Many designers are reporting a significant speedup in the design process as a result of using pictograms as a central tool of design.

Some designers find it useful to design from oversized sheets of paper, or from flipcharts, or from large wall murals. And they tend to use a wide mix of images in the same pictogram.

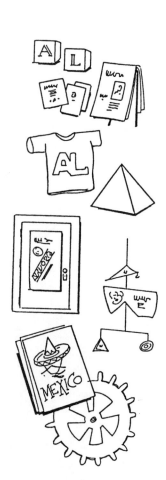

Room Peripherals

Pictograms in the form of wall hangings, murals, or even floor displays can be used as peripherals in the classroom. Care should be taken, however, to make them interesting, attractive, and aesthetically pleasing or they will turn on you. And make sure any lettering is big enough and bold enough to be read from a distance.

Large pictograms can be used for depicting agendas, course objectives, learner benefits, system flows, procedures, and course content of all kinds.

One easy way to create large images for peripherals is first to draw or photocopy the image you want onto an overhead transparency. Project the image onto a poster board or large piece of easel paper. Then trace it with colored pens. In this way, anything you can get onto an overhead transparency, you can get onto the wall or a flipchart in any size and any color you want.

Note Taking

Ask learners to take presentation notes in pictogram form. It will keep them awake during a presentation and allow them to absorb and integrate much more information than if they just sat there gazing vacantly at the presenter. Give them a set of colored pens, a little training in how to make pictograms, and set them loose.

Study Tool

Ask learners to capture the essence of a reading assignment (or an experience) in pictogram form. In most cases it will help them integrate and retain more information. And it will be more fun.

Some graduates of the *Accelerated Learning Training Methods Workshops* who are studying for advanced academic degrees report that by using large pictogram murals as study tools, their learning and recall improves significantly.

To foster *collaborative* learning in the classroom, partners or small teams could create joint pictograms from the material of the course. And their products could be used as room peripherals if appropriate.

You could even sponsor an "art contest" between teams, with each team's pictogram entry judged by everyone in the class on the basis of the four criteria of accuracy, completeness, creativity, and aesthetic beauty.

Pictograms as aids to study are a natural. Whenever people translate information from verbal to pictorial form, much more information sticks.

Presentation Aid

Pictograms can speed the initial input of learning material. They can be used to spice up lectures or used in study guides and reference materials to illustrate and illuminate the verbal text.

Course Map

Provide learners with a large pictogram summarizing an entire course or topic within a course. If you cannot print the course map in color, provide learners with colored pens and ask them to color it themselves. Then they can use it as a reinforcer or a job aid after the course.

Learning Review

Learners, singly or in teams, can create pictograms to review a lesson or an entire curriculum.

Knowledge Assessment

"Shell" pictograms (where people have to fill in the blanks with words and pictures) can be used as a check of learning. They are generally less intimidating than the standard "test" and a lot more fun.

Job Aids

Pictograms of all types can be used for job aids. Learners themselves can create their own pictogram job aids to take with them after the training.

Manuals

Reference manuals can be strengthened by the use of pictograms and icons. Whole icon languages can be developed for illustrating various processes and procedures.

Project Reports

When reporting on projects, you can provide one or more colorful pictograms to supplement and illuminate an otherwise strictly verbal and numeric presentation of information.

Long-Range Planning

Long-range planning can also get a creative boost from the pictogram approach. Pictograms can allow you to create, work with, and display the "big picture" of a long-range plan. They can help you generate ideas, see connections, and easily modify strategies as situations change.

Brainstorming

Pictograms can be useful for all sorts of individual and team-based brainstorming tasks such as:

- problem definition
- problem solving
- product planning
- action planning
- process improvement

Meetings

Pictograms can be used to enhance the effectiveness of meetings. Here are a few applications:

- meeting notices
- agendas
- peripherals
- presentations
- decision-making aids
- action plans
- minutes

Check the Resources section of this book for more information on making and using pictograms.

Examples From the Field

Pictogram Flowchart
Children's Medical Center, Dallas

Penny Williams of Children's Medical Center has transformed the wordy flowcharts for lifesaving procedures into pictograms. The pictograms have been effective as both learning tools and job aids. Here's an example: both pages facing each other contain the same information, but in different formats.

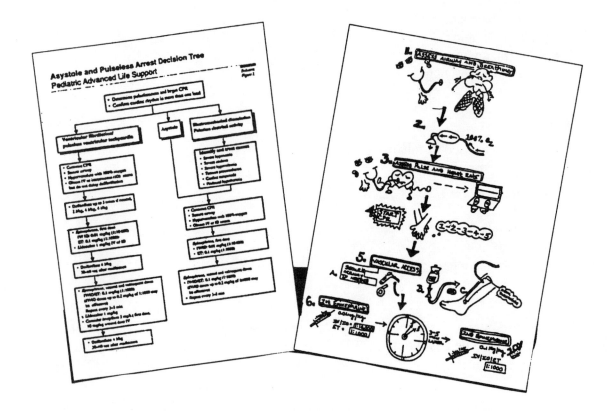

Pictogram Course Maps

Pictogram Course Maps have been used by many A.L. practitioners for many kinds of courses. Here's a sampling.

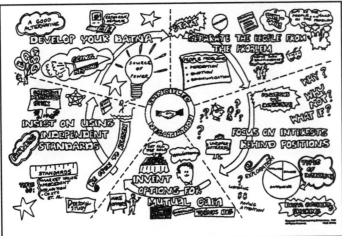

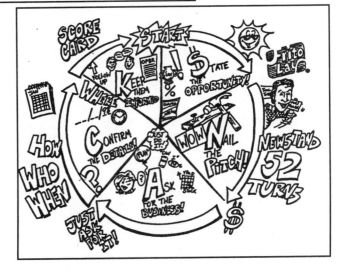

CHAPTER 14

Question-Raising Techniques

Getting Learners to Learn by Asking

The ability to ask questions is a sign of a curious mind and the mark of a good learner. Getting your learners to ask questions ceaselessly will have a positive impact on their learning and their subsequent job performance.

To make learners into ceaseless questioners means that you have to help them overcome years of conditioning. Most people in our culture have been unconsciously conditioned to believe that asking too many questions is a sign of stupidity. It's sometimes embarrassing to admit that we just don't know. So we hesitate to ask too many questions in a classroom setting, assuming that others already know and fearing that by asking too many questions we'll label ourselves as an ignoramus in the eyes of our peers.

Here are some ways that you can inspire learners to enhance their learning by asking any and all of the questions they have. Check the ones that seem most usable to you for a specific learning program. Then go ahead and use them. And invent some of your own.

Intelligence shows itself
not so much
in always having the right
answers but in
being able to ask the
right questions.

1. Question Party

Ask people to stand up and greet everyone in the room as they might at a cocktail party or reception. As two people greet each other, have them ask each other a question about the learning material. It could be a question they know the answer to or a question they don't know the answer to. If it's a question they don't know the answer to and their partner doesn't either, both of them ask a third or a fourth person until they get an answer. After an exchange of questions and answers, each partner finds another person to greet with a question. After this exercise, the facilitator can field any questions that were not answered.

2. Answer Search

Ask people to write 3 or more questions they have about a subject on a piece of paper. Then ask them to rise and wander around the room for 5 minutes or so asking their questions to each other one on one. If the person asked a question does not know the answer either, then the two people should ask a third or a fourth person until they find the answer. Any unanswered questions can be fielded by the facilitator after the exercise. As a review, the facilitator can ask learners to read their questions to the class and disclose the answers they were given. Class members and the facilitator can respond as appropriate.

3. Question Marathon

Put people in pairs. Designate one partner "A" and the other "B." Have "A" ask "B" questions nonstop for five minutes, one question after the other. Questions can be a mix of ones the questioners know the answer to and ones they don't. Have them make note of the questions neither "A" nor "B" can answer. After the allotted time, have the partners exchange roles. After this exercise the class as a whole, together with the facilitator, can field any questions that remained unanswered.

4. Question Post

Give learners several large Post-It notes and ask them to write on each one a question they have about the learning material. Ask them to post their questions anonymously on a question board on the wall or on a flipchart. During a break, ask learners to examine the questions and pick off those that they can answer. After the break, have learners read to the class the questions they have picked and give the answers. Classmates and the facilitator can add to these answers as appropriate. Any questions remaining on the question board after this exercise can be fielded by the facilitator.

5. Question Ball

Give each person a full sheet of blank paper. Ask everyone to write a question that they have on the paper. Ask them to print their question so someone else can easily read it and to not sign their name. Have them ball up the paper. You can then collect the question balls in a bucket and redistribute them by throwing one to every person in the class. Or if the group needs a physical energizer, you can ask them to stand up and have a snowball fight with the question balls, seeing how many people they can hit in 30 seconds. Then, at a signal, ask everyone to pick up a ball, open it, and use any person or resource in the room to help answer the question on it. After a few minutes, ask everyone to read their question to the class and give its answer. The facilitator and the other learners can comment as necessary.

6. Put All Your (Question) Cards on the Table

Distribute blank index cards to learners seated five or six to a table. Ask each learner to write the questions they have about the learning material on the cards, one question per card. Then ask all the people at the table to combine their cards in one deck. Have each table select a dealer. The dealer then shuffles the deck and deals the cards face down to everyone at the table. Each learner in turn reads one of his or her question cards to the group, which is then given 30-60 seconds to answer it. Questions that cannot be answered by the group are placed in the middle of the table and are asked to the whole class at the end of play.

7. Musical Questions

Ask each learner to print a question they have about the learning material on an index card. Ask people to stand and form a circle.

While you play music, ask them to keep passing the question cards around the circle to the person on the right. When the music stops, they'll be given 1-3 minutes to formulate an answer to the question they are holding. They can use any person or resource in the room to help them answer it. Then everyone reads their question and gives its answer.

8.   Hot Potato Question Circle

Ask people to stand and form a circle. Have one of the learners start the play by asking a question and throwing a Koosh ball or other soft ball to anyone in the circle. The person catching the ball has to answer the question. If the person cannot answer the question immediately, they quickly throw the ball like a hot potato to someone else in the circle. The ball keeps circulating until someone can answer the question posed. The person answering the question gets to ask a new question and the process starts all over again. Instead of a Koosh ball, you could use an actual potato. (Variation: To prime the pump, the facilitator can give everyone in the circle a card with a question on it to be asked when its their turn.)

9.   Team Question Exchange

Divide the learners into two or more teams. Ask each team to devise a 10- or 20-question quiz for another team that would test their understanding of the learning material. Teams then exchange question sets. The first team to answer all their questions correctly wins a bag of peanuts or some other prize.

10. Question Face-Off

Divide the class into two teams. Have each team create 10 or 20 questions about the learning material for their opposing team. Then have teams stand and fire questions at each other one at a time. If a team can answer the question in an allotted amount of time, they get a point.

11. Stump Your Buddy

In the middle or at the end of a presentation, put people in pairs. Have partners ask each other five questions about the subject matter— both questions they know the answer to and those they don't. If neither partner can answer a question posed, the partners ask this question to the whole group at the end of the exercise.

12. Pass the Hat

Ask everyone to put one or more of their questions on a card and put it in a hat. Then have each learner pull a question from the hat and read it to the class. The first person to answer it correctly gets a point, or a peanut, or a piece of chewing gum, or whatever. The facilitator answers only those questions that none of the learners can.

CHAPTER 15

Learning Games

It is in the midst of play that we are most in possession of our full powers. An unobstructed sense of play releases all sorts of positive endorphins in our bodies, exercises our wholeness, and gives us the sense of being fully alive. For many people the highest expression of life and of the creative intelligence within them is achieved in play. Learning games that create a playful atmosphere and release people's full and unbridled intelligence have a contribution to make.

Learning games, wisely used, can:

- take the inhibiting "seriousness" out of the air
- de-stress the learning environment
- get people totally involved
- improve the learning process

Accelerated Learning does not always require games, and games of themselves do not always accelerate learning, but games used with discretion can add variety, zest, and interest to some learning programs.

Caveat

Like all learning techniques, games are not ends in themselves but only means towards the ends of enhanced learning. Sometimes a game can be interesting, clever, fun, and very engaging, but produces no substantial learning or long-term value. In that case it's just a big waste of time and should be scrapped. The simple rule is this: If games result in enhanced learning and improved job performance, use them. If they don't, don't.

> One of the greatest faults in modern education is overstructuring, which does not allow for play at every point in the educational process.
>
> –Edward T. Hall

Games That Add Value

In order for a learning game to be effective and add real value to the learning process it should:

1. Be related directly to the workplace. The best games are ones that provide knowledge, reinforce attitudes, and initiate action essential for success on the job.

2. Teach people how to think, access information, react, understand, grow, and create real-world value for themselves and their organization on a continuing basis.

3. Be as enjoyable and engaging as possible without striking people as being silly or superficial. (Games that appear shallow and childish can turn people off.)

4. Allow for collaboration among learners. (Any competition in a game should be between *teams* and not individuals.)

5. Be challenging, but not to the point of frustration and disconnect.

6. Permit ample time for reflection, feedback, dialog, and integration.

And remember this: **don't overdo it!** Too much of any one thing (games included) can destroy learning effectiveness.

What the Right Game Can Do

The right game for the right audience at the right time can make learning fun and interesting, can provide a helpful review that strengthens the learning, and can even act as a kind of a test and measure of learning.

If games result in enhanced learning and improved job performance, use them. If they don't, don't.

When to Use Games

Games can be used throughout a training event in any of the 4 phases of learning. For example:

Preparation: Team-based or group-based games can be used at the start of a training event to measure

existing knowledge, arouse curiosity, and build interest. Examples:
- team-based quiz games
- scavenger hunts
- problem-solving games

Presentation: Team-based learning games can be used as encounter devices where teams can access the learning materials in the process of answering questions. Examples:
- quiz show games
- question baseball
- 20 questions

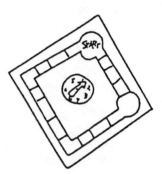

Practice: Games can be used to practice the new knowledge or skill and reinforce the initial learning. Examples:
- quiz show games
- board games
- card games
- unjumble the components
- Pictionary
- Concentration
- Jeopardy
- Family Feud

Performance: Partnered, team-based or individual games can be used to test knowledge or to apply a newly learned skill. Examples:
- question/answer games
- problem-solving games
- information-accessing games
- model-building games

Some Suggested Games

There are many books of learning games on the market. Check the bibliography for a list of some of them. Meanwhile, here are a few ideas for games to start you thinking.

Matching Games

Construct games that test people's ability to match terms with definitions, features with benefits, conditions with responses, questions with answers, etc. This can take many forms and can be individual, partnered, or team-based. You can use a table-top, a wall, a magnetic whiteboard or the floor to display the matches. Game points could be based on speed, accuracy, or both.

Stick the Label on the Component

Give partners or small teams labels containing the names of components of a system. Have them stick the labels on the various components of a system they are studying. Game points could be based on speed, accuracy, or both.

"Name That..." Games

Construct an appropriate preview or review game for the subject you're teaching such as: "Name That Symbol," "Name That Error Message," "Name That Malfunction," "Name That Product," "Name That Communication Technique," or whatever.

Dice Games

Prepare a deck of question cards. Partners or teams take turns picking cards. If a partner or team can answer a question correctly in the allotted amount of time they get to roll the dice, receiving points equal to the role.

Race Games

Similar to Dice Games above with each participant's or team's play piece advancing on a model of a racetrack according to the roll of the dice.

Spinner Games

Create a spinner board with numbers,

colors, or category names around the perimeter. Prepare a deck of cards for each number, color, or category on the spinner board. Partners or teams take turns spinning, answering a question from the deck corresponding to where the needle stopped. A correct answer in the allotted time wins a point.

Hangman

Divide the class into partners. Give each partnership a deck of cards with questions on one side and related answers on the other. Ask partners to shuffle the deck and take turns answering questions. When a partner answers a question incorrectly, he or she must make a hangman mark. The partner who completes the hangman diagram first is the "loser."

Sports-Related Games

For an appropriate audience you can create a game organized around a sports theme: baseball, football, basketball, hockey, soccer, or whatever.

Board Games

Create a board game on a tabletop, on a magnetic wallboard, or on the floor (bigger than life). You can model it after *Monopoly, Trivial Pursuit, Parcheesi,* or other popular game boards. Or create a design of your own. Put together a deck of question cards that test people's knowledge or event cards that reflect real-world situations that people will be faced with. The game can be individual-, partner-, or team-based, whatever is most appropriate.

TV Game Shows

Games based on TV game shows have been popular. Games such as *Jeopardy, Family Feud, Concentration, Beat the Clock,* and others, can easily be adapted to any content.

Computer-Based Games

Games played on a computer can be useful in both classroom and distance learning environments. One example is software called *Quiz Show*, a suite of games (including a Jeopardy-type and a Tic-Tac-Toe game) that allows you to input question sets easily for play between partners and teams. Check the *Resources* section of this book to find out how you can obtain a copy of *Quiz Show*.

20 Questions

Give each partnership or team the same list of 20 questions. The first partnership or team to answer all the questions correctly wins.

Reconstruction

Construct an entire system, process, or procedure out of poster board components on a tabletop, mag board, or on the floor. Jumble the components up. Then have partners or teams put the components back into the correct configuration while explaining out loud what they're doing and why. The group that accomplishes this the fastest wins.

Have Learners Create Games

As a learning exercise, ask a team of learners to create a game that will help people review and retain course content. Then play the game with the group.

Special Note on Quiz Questions

Questions in a question/answer game need not always require quick short answers, but can pose problems to solve that may take more time. Other questions may be "open book" and exercise people's information-accessing skills, timing how long it takes them to find the answers in the documentation.

Examples From the Field

Golf Game
Commonwealth Edison

Bob Anderson of Commonwealth Edison in Chicago invented a golf game for reviewing technical procedures in a nuclear plant. He created question cards and labeled them 100-yard, 200-yard, and 250-yard questions by degree of difficulty.

He divides the class into teams of four. Each "foursome" in turn selects a question of desired difficulty. If they answer it correctly, they move their player the appropriate amount of yardage on the fairway. (The fairways are projected onto a magnetic whiteboard from an overhead transparency. Each foursome's playing piece is magnetized.)

To make things more interesting, foursomes have to pick a card from an accompanying deck that tells them if their ball landed on the fairway, in the rough, or in one of the traps. When a team's ball

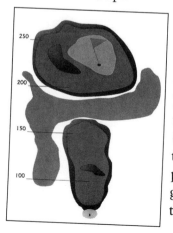

lands on the green, they draw a card from another deck that indicates how far from the pin they are (from one to ten feet). Using a portable putting green set up in the room, one of the team members then has to put the ball in the cup, adding the number of strokes it takes to the team's total score. After five holes, the winning team is announced. Then the learners are tested on the procedures through both written and hands-on evaluations.

Bob says that using the game has had "tremendous results" in improving test scores. And learners' reactions have been "nothing but positive." They enjoy the hands-on nature of the game. And answering the questions, since it involves both collaboration and rigorous thought, helps them learn the procedures more durably.

Spinner Review Game
Florida Power & Light

Sherri Jones and Sue Kelleher came up with a generic spin-the-bottle game that works for almost any content. They placed pieces of poster board on the floor in a circle, each piece labeled with one of the topics covered in the training session. After dividing the class into teams, the teams took turns spinning an oversized plastic Coke bottle. When the bottle stopped, the facilitator read a question from a prepared list relative to the topic the bottle pointed to. If the team answered correctly in under a minute, they got to roll a pair of oversize dice and move their piece on a large *Chutes and Ladders* game board. The winning team was the one who successfully got through the game board first.

Sucker Ball Review Game
Eastman Chemical Company

Laurie Watson divides her class into small teams. With everyone standing, she reads review questions one at a time and asks the teams in turn to answer them within a specified time. A correct answer gives the team a chance to earn some play money.

Ahead of time, Laurie had drawn circles with numbers in them on the whiteboard, a large circle having a small number and a small circle having a large number. After a correct answer, a team member stands at a line 15 feet from the whiteboard and throws a sucker ball (a toy ball covered with small suction cups) at the numbered circles. Whatever number is hit, that's how much play money the team earns.

When all the review questions are answered, team members have a chance to spend what they earned at the "In-Class Quick Mart" — a table set up with snacks (fruit, nuts, candy) and small prizes, all labeled with price tags. (The prices are inflated, of course. A banana may cost $5.) The learners go shopping, take a break, and then move on to the next topic.

Basketball Learning Game
Southern California Edison

Mike Colonese used a basketball theme in a technical review course for Operators at the San Onofre Nuclear Generating Station on the California coast. Learners entered a room decorated like a basketball court. A junior basketball net stood at the front of the room. NBA banners decorated the walls. An NBA video was playing. Small nerf-type basketballs were handed to the learners as they entered with the invitation to take practice shots. When everyone arrived, the group was divided into two teams. Each team then elected its captain.

Mike, dressed in a referee's shirt with a whistle around his neck explained the rules of the learning game. He had provided three stacks of questions about the topic of the day on a table at the front, each stack labeled with a number (1, 2, and 3) indicating the degree of difficulty of the question. For each of the four

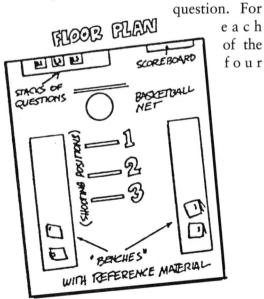

quarters of play the teams picked five questions, mixing the degree of difficulty any way they chose. Then at the whistle, each team had five minutes to research the answers to their questions using documentation and calculators at their "benches."

Then the play began. Teams took turns reading their questions one at a time and giving their answers. If the answer was correct, the captain stood before the net at a mark on the floor corresponding to the difficulty of the question (1 being close and 3 being the furthest away) and took a shot. If the captain sank the shot, the team was given the corresponding number of points which were posted on a computer-controlled scoreboard in the room. Back and forth it went between the teams until all five questions for that quarter were addressed.

Then the team picked another set of five questions for the second quarter and repeated the process. And so it went for four quarters of play. The collaboration among teams, the competition between the teams, and the atmosphere of play turned a sleeper course into a significant learning experience.

Football Learning Game
GM - Allison Transmission

The 2-day operator training course for reading gauges on the shop floor at Allison Transmission is serious business. It costs time and money every time an operator misreads a gauge.

The course material is tedious, requiring learners to solve challenging mathematical problems. It's too critical to have fun with, everyone thought. Learners were used to dragging themselves through a slow and painful learning experience.

Not anymore. Ed Major and Jeff Robinette changed all that. They redesigned the course using a football theme to give it some pizzaz and improve the learning.

Learners are sent a ticket ahead of time that they must use to gain admittance to the game. The excitement starts the minute they arrive. NFL banners are hanging about. A large football field game board and scoreboard are on the wall. Enlarged mock-ups of the various shop-floor gauges hang from the ceiling. Jeff, the instructor, is wearing a referee's uniform. There are 8 different work-stations around the room, each with one of the 8 gauges people will be learning how to use.

The morning is used to prepare for the big game. The various gauges are explained and demonstrated. Hypothetical scenarios are worked through. People ask questions and engage in detailed discussions.

The afternoon is kick-off time for the game. People are put in pairs and given a football helmet magnet which they put at their starting position on the football field. The partners have to visit all of the eight work-stations, one by one, in any sequence. Each station has a stack of ten problem cards that the pair has to work through using the gauge at that station. The referee judges the answers they come up with. For every right answer, they draw a Gainer Card which tells them how much yardage they've gained. They move their playing piece accordingly on the football field. An incorrect answer gives them a Penalty Card that specifies lost yardage.

Learners circle the room until they work through all the problem cards. Along the way they are gaining and losing yards and scoring touchdowns. After each touchdown, learners get a chance to physically kick a nerf football through a goal post in the room for an extra point. The winner is the team with the most points.

Ed and Jeff say that the fun, the working in teams, and the friendly competition among teams gives the course new energy.

Learners never showed any signs of tiredness or slowing down, even in the afternoon. And because they were, in effect, teaching each other, it took a lot of pressure off the instructor.

CHAPTER 16

Imagery
and Learning

Imagery is another important tool that helps improve the speed and durability of learning. Imagery can be auditory, visual, physical, or internal and it can take many forms such as:

- Graphics (pictures, symbols, icons)
- Metaphors and analogies
- Physical objects
- Mnemonic (memory) devices
- Stories
- Body language
- Rhythmic jingles
- Multisensory mental imagery

> The soul never thinks
> without a picture.
>
> –Plato

The Gutenberg Revolution

Imagery of all kinds played a big role in human learning throughout history. But in the 1440s something happened to change all that: the invention of the printing press by Johannes Gutenberg. Ever since, Gutenberg's invention has had a profound effect on Western education.

One result of the printing press was that it elevated words over images. Producing images was very labor intensive, but words could be assembled and printed quite easily. Books of words, then, became the main method of information transfer and the primary vehicle for education.

Another result of the printing press was that it elevated the left brain over the right, since words require linear, sequential processing unlike images which require more simultaneous, holistic processing.

Still another result is that books of words permitted people to

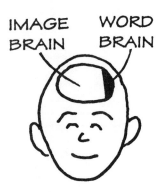

IMAGE BRAIN   WORD BRAIN

learn by themselves off-line through reading rather than on-line through social interaction and trial-and-error immersion in the real world. Word-based learning, then, elevated verbal abstraction over concrete experience.

The printing press continues to have a strong, subconscious hold on all of our educational beliefs and practices. Even as we enter the Internet Age, words are king.

The Power of Images

Images are more potent messengers of meaning than words alone. This is because the human brain is basically an image processor, not a word processor. The part of the brain used to process words is tiny compared with the part of the brain used to process images of all kinds (visual, auditory, olfactory, gustatory, kinesthetic, emotional, etc.). That's why the brain *prefers* images over words. Images are concrete and therefore instantly memorable. Printed words are abstract and much harder for the brain to hold on to.

Today the whole education and training infrastructure is over-Gutenbergized and ververbalized to the point of gross ineffectiveness. It's common, for instance, for training professionals to use flipcharts, overhead transparencies, computer screens, and PowerPoint presentations loaded with words. When it's all over, not much sticks. And because little gets remembered, even less gets acted upon.

The right kind of images, on the other hand, can help concretize the abstract and make learning more direct, effective, and durable.

> The brain is mainly an image processor, not a word processor.

Images: Energy Efficient Learning

Your brain absorbs and stores images instantly and automatically— sights, sounds, smells, tastes, feelings, and all the rest. Think of it. You can easily recall your evening meal last night in great detail or one of the best vacations you ever had. You can, through imagery, relive thousands of experiences you've had throughout your life. When you were having these experiences you were never concerned about memorizing any of them. Your image brain was doing it for you automatically, and on many levels simultaneously.

That's why image-rich experience can teach you much more in less time and with less effort than words alone ever could.

Great teachers through the ages have known this. They have been masters of imagery. They've used stories, metaphors, parables, physical objects, bodily movement, and concrete examples to indelibly etch their teaching in people's minds. We have a great deal to learn from them.

Words are vastly important too. I'm not in any way suggesting that words be abandoned. Not at all. What I am suggesting is that we bring imagery up to a parity with words in our learning programs. This is bound to have a positive effect on everyone's learning.

Imagery Research

Research verifies the power of imagery in learning. Several years ago with a grant from the U.S. Government, Dr. Owen Caskey of Texas Tech University and I did a year-long study on the effect of imagery on learning. Participating in the study were 264 college students from four different types of schools across the U.S. In this study, the people who used imagery to learn scientific and technical information did on average 12% better on immediate recall and 26% better on long-term retention of the information. These averages held for all participants regardless of their age, ethnicity, grade-point average, gender, or learning style.

A controlled study at Travelers Insurance had even more astonishing results. In teaching a new computerized claim processing program to claim adjusters, the groups that worked together to create and use imagery to remember the learning material scored more than 400% better on the qualifying exam than the groups who were not encouraged to collaborate on creating and using imagery to learn.

> Imagery is the highest form of mental energy we have. Reason can analyze and organize, but only the imagination can create.

Types of Images

Imagery can take many forms: graphics, metaphors, physical objects, mnemonic devices, stories, body language, and internal mental imagery. Let's explore each of these briefly.

Graphics

Pictures, icons, and symbols can help make the abstract concrete. (Look at what icons have done for computers.) Here are just a few suggestions of what you could do:

Various Forms and Uses of Graphic Images

- Depict concepts, terms, and processes in vivid, colorful pictures, photographs, and images on overheads and in PowerPoint presentations.

- Give learners a pictogram map of the entire learning program or of a central topic within it.

- Give learners time to complete a partially filled out pictogram with information they gather from a presentation, a computer tutorial, or from written material.

- Ask learners to make their own colorful pictograms out of what they are learning.

- Create colorful peripherals for the learning environment that depict the subject matter graphically.

- Include icons and graphic illustrations in manuals, computer-based programs, and other learning materials.

- Ask learners to create their own icon-based job aids.

Some additional suggestions:

- If you use an overhead projector, you can have colored prints made into 8½" x 11" transparencies on a color copier and display them as part of your presentation.

- Try not to overuse commercial clip art. Some clip art can

have an unimaginative, institutional, same-old-same-old look to it and thus lose its effectiveness. (For some variety, check the *Resources* section for information on hand-drawn, noncommercial-looking clip art for accelerated learning.)

- Here's a simple idea for enhancing a drawing or photo. Expand it on a copier to the size you want. Place a clear overhead over it and trace it with colored transparency pens. This will warm up the graphic and give it a friendly hand-drawn (rather than machine-made) look.

Look for more ideas on using graphics in the *Pictograms* chapter.

It is necessary only to be master of the metaphor.
—Aristotle's advice to teachers

Metaphors and Analogies

When helping people grasp an idea or concept, use the known to illuminate the unknown. Look for ways to illustrate new concepts by comparing them with something that people are already familiar with in nature or in routine life. Some examples are:

- Sending electrical current through a wire is like sending water down a hose. With the spigot and the right hose attachment, you can vary the speed, volume, and force. The same with electricity.

- Getting people to talk about what they just learned is like issuing a SAVE command on a computer. It helps them integrate and internalize the new material. Otherwise, everything you put on their screen is lost.

- Call handling in a large-scale telephone system works the same way an amusement park works in queuing up people for the various rides.

Physical Objects

Often physical objects can help make the abstract concrete. Ask yourself: "If I were teaching this subject to people who had a minimal command of the language, how could I present the ideas and concepts using physical objects?" Go to a garage sale, a toy store, a craft shop, or a novelty store and use your imagination to find something that will work. Or invent your own objects out of common items or craft materials.

- Use toys, household items, natural objects, or hand puppets to describe a concept, process, or system.

- Create an integrated model of a system or process on a tabletop or on the floor using craft materials, toys, legos, and other three-dimensional objects. Or construct a two-dimensional model on a mag board out of pieces of mag-backed materials.

- Wear a costume and act out a concept central to the learning. You could play the role of an irate customer in a customer service class or an incompetent supervisor in a management class. In a computer class you could wear a sandwich board with a replica of a computer screen on it and play the role of a new piece of software as you explain yourself in the first person to the learners. Using this same sandwich board approach, you could be a piece of equipment, a new process, a form, a key concept, an idea, or just about anything.

Mnemonic (Memory) Devices

You can use mnemonic (neh-món-ic) devices throughout a learning program to help people remember key information. (*Mnemonic*, by the way, is the Greek word for *memory*.) Mnemonic devices can take the forms of rhymes, acronyms, physical movements, acrostics, and more.

- The acronym ROY G. BIV help people remember the colors in the light spectrum in their proper order: <u>R</u>ed, <u>O</u>range, <u>Y</u>ellow, <u>G</u>reen, <u>B</u>lue, <u>I</u>ndigo, and <u>V</u>iolet.

- The nuclear industry uses the acronym STAR to help operators remember how to approach any problem in a nuclear plant: <u>S</u>top, <u>T</u>hink, <u>A</u>ct, and <u>R</u>eview.

- The rhyme "Righty-Tighty, Lefty-Loosey" will always remind you of how light bulbs, screwdrivers, bolts, and most valves work.

- Once you know that there's <u>A RAT</u> in SEP<u>ARAT</u>E, you'll never misspell that word.

- And who could live without "i after e except after c?"

- Ask the learners themselves to come up with ways of remembering the various terms, processes, and concepts they're learning about and share their bright ideas with each other.

Stories

From ancient times, stories have been the most widely used mnemonic device. Stories are a series of linked images that appeal directly to the image brain. They are one of the best methods you could ever use to make the abstract concrete and, therefore, memorable.

Stories can be used to illustrate:

- How a technique or methodology has been successfully (or unsuccessfully) applied.

- How an order is processed through a system.

- How various manufacturing processes work. (The story could be told from the point of view of the item being manufactured.)

- Successful books like *The One-Minute Manager* and *Zapp* present their ideas in story form. The right kind of story can add human interest to an otherwise dry subject and thus aid the learning.

Body Language

You can use your body to illustrate the ideas you are presenting. Facial expressions, exaggerated gestures, and bodily movement can give people a concrete picture of what you're talking about.

- When talking about eliminating some negative attitude or practice from the workplace, you could mime dropping a dead skunk into a garbage can while you hold your nose and exclaim: "Yechh!"

- When describing digital to analog conversion you could first illustrate digital by walking across the room very mechanically in up and down jerks while exclaiming "Up, down, up, down" or "On, off, on, off." Then to illustrate analog, you could walk across the room in a loose, wave-like flow while making musical sounds.

- You could illustrate sales resistance by holding both your arms out toward the audience with your open palms facing them and a sour look on your face. To illustrate acceptance, you could hold your arms out as they would be just prior to a welcoming embrace while your eyes light up and your face beams a bright smile.

Multisensory Mental Imagery

Because the human mind is more of an image processor than a word processor, mental imagery can be a powerful addition to any learning program. Again, mental imagery is not only what you can imagine seeing, but what you can imagine hearing, touching, feeling, tasting, smelling, and doing as well.

The use of mental imagery in education and training was more or less banished during the industrial era. But it came roaring back into the culture in the 1970s when it got applied to sports training. Now many athletes use mental imagery on a regular basis to improve their performance.

End-result imagery.

Have learners sit quietly and imagine a positive end result related to what they are learning. Salespeople, for instance, can imagine the perfect sales call. Customer Service Reps can imagine doing their job successfully. Managers can imagine a current problem already solved. People who have to create something can see it in their imagination as already created. After doing the imagery, ask everyone to talk with a partner about their experience and what they learned from it. They can then share these experiences with the whole group as appropriate.

Imaginary voyage.

People can imagine themselves miniscule in size as they travel through a system or process. For example, medical people can take a "fantastic voyage" through livers, lungs, or circulatory systems as part of the learning process. Design engineers can put themselves inside the systems they're designing. Others can imagine themselves traversing telephone systems, manufacturing operations, processes in a power plant— whatever they are learning about. Again, after a brief imagery experience, have partners talk with each other about what they observed and what they can learn from it.

Skill rehearsal.

Imagery can be used to rehearse any skill, from tennis to public speaking. One telephone company uses imagery as part of their pole climbing training program. Another company has trainees operate a chemical washing plant in their minds before they do it in reality.

Guided Imagery Guidelines

When creating guided imagery scenarios to be used either live or on audiotape, here are some guidelines.

1. You can use guided imagery to introduce a subject, but most often you will use it as a presentation, practice, and performance activity once people are into a subject.

2. When designing guided imagery scenarios, use your wildest imagination. Think like a child. Play. Ask yourself, "How would I teach this subject if I wanted to get people totally involved and had all the time and money in the world?" Figure that out, then do just that in the imagination.

3. Use simple language. Avoid wordiness. Speak in the present tense.

4. Prior to the imagery, bring learners into a relaxed and open state by playing soft, relaxing music, dimming the lights, doing a relaxation exercise— all or any combination of these.

5. An imagery scenario can range in time from a matter of seconds to 5-10 minutes. The time allotted will depend on the nature of the subject and the energy level of the participants. With a longer imagery scenario, it may be a good idea to break it up into shorter segments with some learner reflection and processing (talking, writing, drawing) in between.

6. When designing a guided imagery scenario, try to get as many senses involved as possible. Have learners see, touch, taste, smell, and feel.

7. Speak with a calm, natural, unhurried voice. With some exceptions, avoid dramatic tone. And don't be afraid of silence, of pauses. Pauses are important to allow learners time to form and to experience their imagery. The number and length of pauses, of course, will depend on the subject matter of the imagery scenario and what you are trying to accomplish with it.

8. Resist the temptation to guide your learners too specifically. Allow them the freedom to form their own precise images, to have their own unique experiences, and to draw their own conclusions.

9. Allow time after the imagery session for learners to talk with a partner or small team about their imagery experience, to analyze it, draw out implications, and apply it to the learning objectives at hand. Debrief with the whole group as appropriate.

10. Tape record your guided imagery scenario if you like. Then go through it yourself, making note of improvements you could make in content, sequence, tone, speed, length of pauses, and so forth. Rerecord the tape as needed. If the fidelity of the tape is high, you can use it in the classroom. This will give you a bit of a rest. If the tape is not high quality, it would be better to read your scenario live.

CHAPTER 17

Natural Light

Dark Ages

So many training rooms encapsulate people in sterile environments devoid of natural light and separated from contact with the natural world. This can have a negative effect on one's spirit, health, and learning ability.

Natural light is full spectrum light, whereas the artificial light of the fluorescent bulbs that illuminate most office buildings and training rooms produce a much narrower spectrum of light. And fluorescents pulse— even though you're not consciously aware of it (although your body is). The combination of the narrow spectrum light and the constant pulsing can create stress and add to fatigue if a person is denied access to natural light for extended periods of time. In a sense, dark ages you.

The Prussians, who had an influence on American public education at the time of its inception believed, being extremely linear thinkers, that people could only do one thing at a time. They therefore taught that classroom windows create distractions and should be eliminated or shaded to prevent people from looking out and getting offtrack.

American architects and business leaders must have picked up on this, since so many corporate training rooms have been designed without windows or with the windows heavily shaded.

Lighten Up

There has been a fair amount of research indicating that exposure to natural light has a positive effect on human health and emotional well-being. Even on learning.

A study sponsored by the California Board for Energy Efficiency and Pacific Gas and Electric showed that students in rooms with windows and skylights learned faster and scored higher on standardized tests than those in rooms without windows or rooms that were poorly lit.

The research was conducted in three school districts (Capistrano, CA; Seattle, WA; and Fort Collins, CO) and involved 750 classrooms and 21,000 students.

The study found that students in classrooms with the most daylight learned 20-26 percent faster than students in classrooms with the least light. Districtwide averages increased by 8.8 points in reading and 12.5 points in math in bright rooms as opposed to dim ones.

Another study conducted in two first-grade classrooms in Sarasota, FL, by the Environmental Health and Light Research Institute found that full-spectrum light reduced nervousness and hyperactive behavior in the children and improved overall classroom performance.

Dimming Down Is Dumbing Down

Perhaps it's no accident that we refer to an intelligent person as "bright" and an unintelligent person as "dull." Both brightness and dullness, however, can be affected by the environment.

If you ever attended a big conference or a training event where you're kept inside all day under artificial light and the room is dimmed repeatedly for interminable PowerPoint presentations, you know how this can often leave you exhausted and depressed. We're like plants. Light is essential for our health and growth.

Obviously we need to illuminate people in more ways than one if they are to learn at their best.

Let There Be Light

Open those curtains! Pull up those shades! Brighten the environment! But if you're stuck in a room without natural light, as many of us often are, here are a couple things you can do.

Build in learning exercises that take people into light. Have teams or partners work outside for brief periods from time to time, or anywhere inside where there's light — hallways, offices, cafeterias, wherever.

If you're stuck in a room with fluorescents, scatter table lamps and floor lamps around the room for incandescent illumination. Incandescent bulbs have a wider spectrum of light than fluorescents and are thus emotionally warmer and less stressful. (Garage sales and secondhand stores are a wonderful source of inexpensive lamps of all kinds, if you're interested.)

In a windowless room illuminated by fluorescents, replace the cold white tubes with full spectrum ones, and have them installed with radiation shields.

You Need Not Overdo It

You can carry everything too far, including this business of light. A bright room is not going to make you an instant genius, and a dim room is not going to make you an idiot, but a properly lit environment, together with many of the other A.L. touches, can contribute to physical and emotional health and make a positive contribution to learning.

CHAPTER 18

Aromas

Nasal Intelligence

Your nose knows and is negatively disposed if a learning environment doesn't make good scents.

If it smells like whatever, it probably is whatever. You can't fool the nose.

The olfactory part of your brain is very ancient and very wise, having evolved early on as a way of distinguishing good from bad.

It still functions that way. The nose is a significant part of our sensory awareness. We still talk about people having a nose for things, about something that doesn't smell right, about situations that stink, about not being able to get something past your nose. Ancient wisdom.

The olfactory bulbs that process smell are located in the limbic system, the part of the brain that also deals with memory. That's why you can get a whiff of a fragrance that you smelled when you were seven years old and the whole gestalt of that time and place comes rushing back.

And when you walk into a learning environment that has been neglected and smells musty or, in the case of many over-the-hill hotels, has fifteen years of food droppings rotting in the carpet, you know you don't want to be there. But if you have to be there, you feel suddenly dehumanized, punished, uncared for. It's a rotten situation to find yourself in— you feel like garbage. And you're absolutely right. Trust what your nose is telling you. You ARE being treated like garbage. The whole environment, you included, is of a piece with that carpet. It's a flagrant fragrant violation and you know it. A bad aroma makes the whole situation stink.

Fragrance and Learning

There is still a great deal of research to be done on the effects of fragrance on learning. But here's one piece of it.

Dr. Alan Hirsch of the Smell and Taste Research Foundation in Chicago reported on a study he did with students in a high school calculus class in Portland, Oregon. He found that students exposed to a floral aroma during test taking improved their scores from 14% to 54%. There is something to this, no doubt, although the figures seem extreme. But since this research has not been replicated, as far as I know, we have to exercise a little caution before we let the chemical companies offer expensive "Sniff This for Better Grades" products to our children.

Aromatherapy

There is something quite legitimate about the whole aromatherapy approach as long as it doesn't allow itself to get overblown into THE ONE GREAT ANSWER for health and happiness. Yet, fragrances can have a positive effect on mental processing as we all know from experience.

Citrus smells, they say, can give people a sense of freshness and promote mental awareness. Vanilla aromas can be relaxing. Cinnamon can add to a feeling of festivity and benevolence.

When working with trainers at NASA, some of them found that a boiling pot of cinnamon/apple potpourri near the classroom door seemed to please the learners and put them in a good mood.

Here is a brief list of various aromas and their imputed characteristics according to one leading aromatherapist:

BASIL   uplifting, clarifying, awakening, stimulating

CARNATION   secretiveness, stillness, originality, liberation

CINNAMON	warming, secular, fair-minded
CORIANDER	enlivening, motivating, encouraging
GERANIUM	balancing, healing, uplifting, ` comforting
GRAPEFRUIT	radiating, cheerful, liberating
JASMINE	euphoric, sensuous, welcoming, intuitive
LAVENDER	harmonious, calming, healing, compassion
LEMON	purifying, stimulating, clarity, concentration
NARCISSUS	hypnotic, empowering, visionary, creative
ORANGE	warming, happy, resolute, sunny, energizing
PEPPERMINT	clarifying, awakening, stimulating, refreshing
PINE	simplicity, patience, accepting, trusting
ROSEMARY	vigorous, strengthening, restorative
SANDALWOOD	enlightening, balancing, connecting
THYME	empowering, assisting, invigorating

More detail on these and other aromas and their attributes can be found in Valrie Ann Worwood's book, *The Fragrant Mind*.

Don't Overdo It

Too much of anything turns into its opposite. And too much specially applied aroma in a training room can prove to be toxic to some people and make them want to gag. It's the same way you feel when you're standing next to a man doused with far too much after-shave lotion, or a woman with far too much perfume on, or a dog that's just rolled around in its favorite something on the ground. Yechh! A little is attractive, but a lot is repulsive (except for the dog, of course, where even a little is repulsive as far as you are concerned).

The rule is this with aromas: when you want to stop breathing and get out of there, it's been overdone.

So, when you apply aromas to a learning environment, use a gentle touch— a scented candle here or there, a faint spray, a subtle arrangement of potpourri, some fragrant, fresh-cut flowers, a plugin. Nothing too overpowering.

PART 5

Computers and Accelerated Learning

Using Technology Wisely

> "Technology makes an excellent
> servant, but an appalling master."
> —anonymous

Looking for Technological Saviors

Technology has made us wealthy. It is not yet apparent that it has made us wise.

Yet, our society couldn't function for a minute without technology, particularly without computers. Computers and the World Wide Web (still in its infancy) are here to stay and are having a profound effect on human culture on many levels. But to believe that computers are the salvation of education is muddleheaded. It's just another indication of how far over the edge our culture has gone in esteeming technological control over all forms of social, emotional, spiritual, and ecological intelligence.

There is a very legitimate use for computers in education and training. They, like paper, pencils, books, videos, and all the rest, will increasingly become a natural part of most learning environments. For some people and some subjects and some situations, computers are already proving to be effective aids to learning. And the World Wide Web — what a marvel, and what an unbelievably wonderful information resource it is! But to ask the computer (whether local or on the Web) to take over education and training as the ultimate substitute teacher is to ask it to do something it's incapable of.

The term "cyberspace" was coined by William Gibson in his 1984 novel *Neuromancer.* He defined it as "consensual hallucination."

Automating the 19th Century

In most cases, today's computers make lousy substitute teachers. This is because our computer technology has advanced rapidly while our understanding of human learning has stayed firmly glued to the 19th century. We simplistically use computers to wrap our outmoded understanding of learning in new technological clothing and call it progress. But by merely applying 21st-century technology to 19th-century assumptions about learning, all we really do is automate our ignorance and allow ourselves to get dumber faster and with greater efficiency.

One example: In corporations, death by overhead has been replaced by death by PowerPoint. Nothing has changed but the technology. The underlying assumptions about learning remain the same. And the mass production of unconscious, comatose audiences remains the same. Now we can put people to sleep technologically rather than manually. Progress.

Another example: As machine-mediated delivery has evolved from teaching machines to CD-ROM to the Web, we've maintained the same basic assumptions about learning– namely that a training program, no matter what the media, is something done **TO** learners and that it's essential to have a controlled medium from which the learner can consume predigested information. The fact that so few people would argue with these assumptions is an indication of how entrenched they are.

The Limits of Technology

Computers and the Web *can* play a big role in learning when used appropriately. But here are some additional factors that make our mechanical schoolmasters less than perfect teachers for everything across the board.

1. Computers tend to be isolating.

All attempts at machine-mediated learning in the past (the teaching machine, the video disk, computer-based training, etc.) have not lived up to their promoter's promises. Why? People found them too socially isolating. According to the research, people learn best not in isolation but by interacting with others in a real-world context.

2. Computers tend to keep people physically passive.

The people who are putting together technology-driven learning programs today tend to still treat learning as a verbal, linear, rationalistic, "head" sort of thing and seem unaware of all the research into the body's role in learning. By not getting people *physically* involved, CBT (computer-based training) and WBT (Web-based training) utilize only a fraction of a person's total resources.

3. Computers tend to appeal to only one learning style.

Some people can sit and learn through computers just fine. But the majority of people who are hands-on, physical, nonlinear learners often find many forms of computer-based learning slow, boring, and ineffective.

4. Computers tend to be media-based rather than experience-based.

CBT and WBT tend to be driven by the technology itself, often substituting learning by media for learning by experience, thus making the virtual world more important than the real one.

Changing Our Beliefs About Learning

Changing our technology without changing our beliefs about learning can result in an incredible waste of resources. Here are some outmoded beliefs about learning that seem to hold sway over Web-based course design. Each is followed by a counterassumption that, in my view, may be more appropriate and yield better results.

Old Belief	New Belief
1. Learning is the absorption of information.	Learning is the creation of meaning, value, and actionable knowledge by the learner.
2. Learning is an individualistic endeavor.	Learning improves greatly in a social environment rich in collaboration and human interaction.
3. Knowledge is mainly verbal and cognitive.	Knowledge involves the whole body/mind, the emotions, the senses, and all aspects of intelligence.
4. Standardization saves time and money.	One-size-fits-all solutions waste money. Learning works best in an option-rich, multipathed environment.
5. We must test for immediate recall as part of learning the program.	Long-term performance, not immediate recall, is the aim of learning.
6. Learning requires a controlled delivery system.	Learning is hampered by too much structuring and too much external, hierarchical control.
7. Learning is serious business.	Learning is best when done in the spirit of joy and playfulness.

How to Use Computers Effectively

Here are some suggestions for using computer technology more effectively as an adjunct to learning. Computers serve best when they help create learning environments that are:

1. **Collaborative.** All good learning is social. Peer teaching, according to a Stanford University study, far outperformed computer tutorials or any other form of instruction. By creating learning programs for teams of two or more people (rather than just for individuals), you can tap into the power of dialog and peer teaching that has proven to enhance the quantity and quality of learning for everyone.

2. **Futzy.** Futzing around with something is the best way to start learning about it. I'm not suggesting that we abandon all structure. Not at all. But good learning programs should not try to overcontrol the learning process, but allow the learner time to futz, to play, to explore, and to experiment. According to Paul Strassmann in his book *The Squandered Computer* (p. 124), research has indicated that people learn better by experimenting, asking coworkers for help, and following menu prompts than they do from highly controlled computer-based tutorials, lecture-driven seminars, or videotaped presentations.

3. **Option-Rich.** The computer should never be thought of as the master teacher and the sole delivery system for learning, but just one component in a whole suite of resources. Chapter 21 in this book will show you how to create an option-rich learning environment for people, making the computer not a one-dish meal, but simply one item in a complete learning smorgasbord.

4. **Activity-Based.** People generally learn more from activities and real-world experiences than they learn from presentations (whether delivered by lecturers or computers). How can we use computers, then, to get learners away from computers and into the real world for live experiences?

5. **Problem-Centered.** Rather than using the computer as a know-it-all information hose, have the computer pose problems for the learners to solve. Problem posing rather than answer-giving gets learners totally involved and teaches them how to

The aim of education should be to convert the mind into a living fountain, not a reservoir.

–John Mason

think, how to search for information, and how to turn information into actionable knowledge– valuable skills in today's world.

6. Creative. Knowledge is not something learners absorb, but something learners create. Computers are used most wisely when they don't simply provide information but help learners create their own meaning, knowledge, and value out of it.

7. 4-Phased. Whether classroom-based or technology-based, organizing a training program around the 4-Phase Learning Cycle (Preparation, Presentation, Practice, Performance) is essential for optimal learning. Designs fail when they emphasize the Presentation Phase to the detriment of the other three phases.

Keeping Learning Human

The whole thrust of technology in the West has been to dehumanize the work environment, substituting machines for human beings wherever possible. It happened in agriculture, in manufacturing, in big business customer service, and now it's happening in training and education. On-Line learning is intended to save lots of money and improve the efficiency of learning by eliminating human beings from the learning delivery process and by making the machine not only an information resource, but a delivery system as well.

Listen to ASTD's introduction to Jay Alden's book, *A Trainer's Guide to Web-Based Instruction*:

> "Increasingly, the transfer of information, knowledge, and skills can be facilitated by a variety of electronic media, often reducing the need for time-intensive transfer based on the interaction of human beings."

There are times when that's true, but as an overall prescription for learning, it's deadly. How can any machine be a substitute for a friend, a coach, a mentor? We've got to give up the notion that, when it comes to training and education, we can flat-out eliminate people, swap in a computer, and have significant human learning take place. Ain't gonna happen.

Several year ago Dr. James F. Wells wrote a scholarly book on the history of Western Civilization called *The Story of Stupidity*. In his concluding remarks he says this:

> "The danger we face is that short-term technological development will continue to enrich society without being balanced by a long-term commitment to the arts and humanities. We will be able to do more and more better and better while forgetting why.

> "Our focus must be on the total human environment for the simple reason that if we insist on evaluating everything simply in terms of immediate technological ability and monetary worth, we will fashion for ourselves only a very efficient and expensive permanent demise.

> "Because of our pride in our technological expertise, we cannot admit that machinery cannot solve our social problems or that computers cannot really educate. The greatest thing we need to learn is how to work with one another to the advantage of all, and no computer can teach us how to do that."

CHAPTER 20

Public Education and the Web

Can Mighty Mouse Save Us?

Technology-based learning is bound to increase over the next few years, simply because the technology is there. The Gartner Group of Stamford, CT, predicts that, in American corporations, the current ratio of 25% technology-based and 75% instructor led training will shift to a 50/50 split by 2002. Some predict the same for schools. Perhaps.

The question is, however, will the greater use of technology in education result in better learning across the board? Some doubt it. Some feel that what we need is not simply a change in technology, but a change in our whole approach to learning. Rewiring our schools and corporations without rewiring our heads will result, they say, in a big waste of time and money.

Yet the hype persists.

In an introduction written by ASTD (the American Society for Training and Development) for Jay Alden's book *A Trainer's Guide to Web-Based Instruction* we read these words:

> "The functionality we looked to build into programmed instruction, teaching machines, and computer-based instruction thrives today on the World Wide Web."

What they fail to mention is that programmed instruction, teaching machines, and computer-based instruction never turned out to be the educational panaceas that their promoters promised. Many feel that the same will prove to be true of the Web.

Teaching is not the application of a system; it is an exercise in perpetual discretion.

–Jacques Barzun, *Begin Here*

The furious stampede of the lemmings to the Net has raised a dust cloud that obscures the questions of how it is improving learning and performance, and what long-term value it is contributing to individuals, the community, and the world. We really don't know yet. But we are admonished not to question the wisdom of our executives, government officials, and computer companies— and just go along with the stampede. Which led William Ruckeyser to remark: "There is so much of an element of blind faith in computer-based learning that demanding evidence of its effectiveness is taken as a sign of heresy."

The Politics of the Web

On February 15, 1996, American politicians Bill Clinton and Al Gore announced their school technology initiative— to wire U.S. schools for the Internet and make all American children computer literate by the year 2000. Since then, some estimates are that $20 billion dollars have been spent and that eventually the price tag will be between $40 and $100 billion. This is certainly a plump windfall for the computer industry, but many serious doubts remain about its value for education.

The Clinton Administration's push for wiring the schools was backed by a presidential (read "rubber stamp") task force composed of industry, education, and special interest groups. All 36 members of the task force were technology advocates who confirmed, without a dissenting voice, the thrust of the Administration's "initiative." McKinsey & Co. wrote their report that cited research indicating greatly improved educational performance using computers.

However, it turns out that much of the research was seriously flawed, lacking the necessary scientific controls. Edward Miller, a former editor of the *Harvard Education Letter* said this:

> "Most knowledgeable people agree that most of the research isn't valid. It's so flawed it shouldn't even be called research. Essentially, it's worthless."

Jane Healy, author of *Failure to Connect: How Computers Affect Our Children's Minds— for Better or for Worse,* agrees. She says:

> "There is poor-to-no evidence that computers teach basic skills better than traditional methods, and poor-to-no evidence that children who don't use computers are somehow "left behind" at a later stage. Conversely, there is abundant evidence that an uncritical infatuation with computers is causing skill building to be replaced with play of an exceptionally formless and mindless sort, while forcing art, music, and even math textbooks off many school budgets."

Obscuring the Real Issues

Larry Cuban, a professor at Stanford University and a one-time school superintendent is author of the book *Teachers and Machines: The Classroom Use of Technology Since 1920.* He was reported in the *New York Times* as saying, "All the hoopla around the Internet obscures the deeper and more important issues of learning, about how do you teach kids to acquire the basic skills and think independently." Todd Oppenheimer in his *Atlantic Monthly* article *The Computer Delusion* (July 1997) quotes Dr. Cuban further: "Schooling is not about information. It's getting kids to think about information. It's about understanding and knowledge and wisdom."

Apple founder Steven Jobs who claims to have "spearheaded giving away more computer equipment to schools than anybody else on the planet" said this in a *Wired* magazine interview when asked about computers in schools:

Repose is not the end of education. Its end is a noble unrest, an ever-renewed awakening from the dead.
–George MacDonald

> "No amount of technology will make a dent...You're not going to solve the problems by putting all knowledge onto CD-ROMs. We can put a Web site in every school— none of this is bad. It's bad only if it lulls us into thinking we're doing something to solve the problem with education."

Joseph Chilton Pearce, author of *Magical Child* is even more pessimistic about technology as the solution for what ails public education. In his book *Evolution's End* he says this:

> "No national 'solution' yet forthcoming has moved beyond a politically motivated or "financially viable" position. The massive thrust for computerized education, capturing the public fancy by design, is a case in point. A computer on every desk, software for the millions and billions for the investors, will be the final straw in damaging children beyond all educability."

Poor Results

It's apparent that we still have much to learn about how to use technology appropriately for public education. So far, all those billions of dollars spent on wiring our schools have had a dismal return on investment.

A survey by *Market Research Retrieval* found that fewer than 14% of American teachers believe the Internet is having a positive impact on student's academic performance.

And in late 1999, *Education Week* magazine released its comprehensive report on technology in schools. It indicated that many teachers don't know what to do with the technology. Almost 50% don't use computers at all in their teaching. And 70% of the high school teachers surveyed said that it is almost impossible to find useful educational products out there. The software programs that are being used are given a grade of C or lower by these teachers.

Sherry Turkle of MIT, a long-term observer of children and computers, has this to say:

> "The possibilities of using this thing (the computer) poorly so outweighs the chance of using it well, it makes people like us, who are fundamentally optimistic about computers, very reticent."

Electronic Baby-Sitting

Many suspect that we are using the computer to replace the old fashioned work sheets (that teachers used to give students to keep them occupied) without questioning and revising our basic assumptions about learning and public education.

What children of all ages need in order to develop their intelligence is not a greater electronic surfeit of disjointed information but whole-body experience in the skill of distilling information into coherent knowledge. Knowledge is something a learner actively creates out of information and experience. It is not a matter of the passive absorption of "facts" through an information medium, be it human or technological. Paulo Freire in his best selling 1970 book *Pedagogy of the Oppressed,* says it well:

> "Knowledge emerges only through invention and reinvention, through the restless, impatient, continuing, hopeful inquiry human beings pursue in the world, with the world, and with each other."

If computers and the Web can help in this pursuit, they have an important contribution to make. If they attempt to be a substitute for this pursuit, they will most certainly fail to bring any positive value to education. Quite the opposite.

"I thought that television would be the last great technology that people would go into with their eyes closed. Now you have the computer.

–Neil Postman,
author of
The End of Education

Technology firms succeed in quest to tap into public education funds

By Douglas D. Noble

Debate about the educational value of computers is largely misdirected, because educational technology has never been about the needs of education, schools, or children. Instead, it has been about powerful corporate interests hawking technological fantasies to schools while in reckless competition over a huge, publicly funded education market.

Most teachers and schools face far more pressing needs and are far too busy to care about, much less learn, new, unwieldy computer applications. And the 35-year track record of computers in schools, including Apple Computer's own 10-year research with the most sophisticated school technologies, reveals precious little contribution to teaching or learning from computer use, despite decades of distraction.

So the urgent demand for technologies in schools is not coming from inside the classroom; it is being orchestrated elsewhere– as it has always been.

In the mid-1960s, the nation's largest technology and publishing firms, scrambling after unprecedented federal funding for education, merged in ill-conceived, computer-based ventures to save education, flooding schools with useless gadgets while ripening them for other such forays in the decades that followed.

Again today, the deal makers behind a flurry of new mergers among telecommunication, technology and entertainment giants are lined up alongside investors eager to reshape and tap a ripe education market. In the words of a recent Lehman Brothers report, "the timing for entry into the market has never been better, as the problems with American education have elevated educational reform to high political priority."

No wonder the latest "educational summits" of the nation's governors, meeting to shape state and national school agendas, have been held at IBM headquarters. High-tech firms have aligned themselves with self-serving politicians, education leaders and even teachers' unions to set educational policies tied to their interests and technologies. And through relentless marketing and ideological battering, they have reduced debate to a mantra of inevitability, securing popular complicity in the siphoning of billions of scarce education dollars.

Internet access, with its unproved benefits for education (as distinct from information, shopping and entertainment) and its expensive fiber-optic infrastructure, is only the last in a long line of inflated corporate strategies pushing computers into schools, all with minimal educational impact.

To be sure, some children benefit from computers in schools, and some parents and teachers have enthusiastically promoted them. But these are hardly the reasons educational computing is once again a high-profile subject on editorial pages. We must turn instead to self-serving corporate and political agendas hard-wiring the nation's schools, with little regard for education or children.

This editorial appeared in USA Today *on April 26, 2000, and is used by permission. It was distilled from an article first published in* Educational Leadership *by Douglas D. Noble, who is a learning specialist with the Learning Development Center at the Rochester Institute of Technology and author of the book* The Classroom Arsenal *(Falmer, 1991).*

CHAPTER 21

Enhancing
Technology-Based Learning

Accelerated learning principles and ideas can greatly enhance all learning, whether local or remote. Most of the ideas in this book that are recommended for classroom use can be applied to computer-based training, Web-based training, satellite-based training, and all forms of distance learning as well. This chapter will give you a ton of ideas for doing just that. But first you need to replace either/or thinking with both/and thinking if you hope to be successful with these ideas.

The Learning Smorgasbord

Ever since Frederick W. Taylor convinced American industrialists that there was one best way to do a specific job, corporate managers have been hoping for a single perfect, technological solution for each challenge that faces them.

In corporations we've seen training managers banging about from one perfect technological solution to the next, following the cycle of "hype, hope, trial, and disappointment" over and over again. Starting after World War II, it was the behavioristic teaching machine that was to revolutionize education and give us effective, efficient learning, then filmstrips and 35mm slides, then CAI (computer-aided instruction), then interactive video, then CBT (computer-based training), then multi-media (CBT with added bells and whistles), then virtual-reality machines.

All of these have failed to live up to the potential promised by their promoters. This was bound to happen because there is no simple, single solution to anything– particularly anything associated with learning. The one-size-fits-all approach has never been effective, is not effective now, and never will be effective.

For every problem there is one solution that is simple, neat, and wrong.

–H.L. Mencken

Variety Is the Spice of Learning

Learning is such a vast and multifaceted human activity that it cannot be controlled by any single medium or method. Rather, all media and all methods can contribute to learning at one time or another in their own way if used appropriately. It would be such a happy, beautiful, and intelligent thing for all of us if we would stop looking for that one-dish meal solution to learning and start thinking in terms of a learning smorgasbord.

The one-dish meal, single-solution approach asks: Should it be classroom or CBT? Should it be CBT or the Web? The Smorgasbord approach on the other hand asks: How can we use a mix of classroom, CBT, the Web, mentoring, and everything else, including stuff we've never thought of yet, to get the job done? How can we provide a wealth of options for people and let them choose their own best path?

No method or media is bad that speeds and enhances learning. No method or media is good that doesn't speed and enhance learning (no matter how "creative" or technologically sophisticated it might be).

True Multimedia

To call a computer with bells and whistles "multimedia" is a misnomer. The computer is still a single medium, no matter how many bells and whistles it has. True multimedia means a wide mix of media ranging potentially from all manner of high-end technology, to a booklet, colored pens, a conversation, a white board, and a whole array of tools and resources.

Artistry, intuition, perspective, and quick emotional and intellectual reflexes are what help teachers survive— not rigid adherence to a particular set of techniques.

–Jonathan Zap,
Holistic Education

The drive to package everything within a CD-ROM or Web program, or any single vessel is madness. It's back to a single medium delivery system. Some day I'm gonna' write a Country and Western song about this and title it:

> "They've Got the Pedal to the Metal,
> but Their Gearshift's in Reverse."

The desire to put everything into one medium is a product of linear, exclusivist, either/or thinking. This type of thinking has plagued training for years and has produced one sterile dogmatism after another.

Once we abandon single-solution, one-dish-meal thinking and adopt a smorgasbord approach, a number of wonderful things happen. We can save a ton of money when we use each piece of media (including the computer and the Web) only for what it's good at. The smorgasbord approach allows us to appeal to a wide range of learning styles, provide people with lots of options, and make learning far more enjoyable and successful for everyone.

Here are just some things you could include in a smorgasbord-type distance learning program to make it truly multimedia:

1. CD-ROM software accessible locally.
2. Software tutorials accessible through the Web.
3. A print media or web-based learning guide.
4. A course map in pictogram form.
5. A set of colored pens for making pictograms.
6. One or more sets of flashcards.
7. A Walkman and audiocassettes.
8. Materials for learning games (dice, game boards, question cards, etc.)
9. Print media learning materials.
10. Colorful job aids.
11. Partially completed forms, templates, and pictograms for taking notes.
12. Manipulatives and 2-dimensional models that learners have to assemble on a tabletop, wall, board, or floor.
13. Cards of procedural steps that learners have to sequence.
14. Peripherals (posters, banners, mobiles) containing learning material.
15. Craft supplies for learners to create their own peripherals.
16. Blank audiotapes to make cassettes out of the learning material.
17. Videotapes containing clips related to the learning material.
18. A list of related Web sites and net-based resources.
19. Names, phone numbers and e-mail addresses of people to contact in the "virtual community" who can help with the learning (teachers, coaches, mentors, peers).
20. Problem-solving exercises to complete.
21. Suggestions for projects related to the learning material.
22. Questions to research on the Web.
23. Board games and computer quiz games loaded with review questions.
24. Lists of scavenger hunt items to be used for information search exercises.
25. Pretest and posttest forms.
26. Books and articles for extra reading.
27. A booklet of suggestions and exercises for partnered learning.
28. Video conferencing equipment and guidelines.
29. Imagery scenarios that guide learners in doing skill rehearsal.
30. Relaxing music to use during imagery sessions and learning exercises.

Now that's multimedia!

*The following training professionals contributed to the above list by pooling their ideas at the July 1999 *Accelerated Learning Training Methods Workshop* in San Francisco:

Cesar de la Fuente, Contido, El Paso, TX; Lisa Jizrawi, Intel, Folsom, CA; Rona Morrow, Missouri Gas Energy, Kansas City, MO; Janice Nord, Nortel, Santa Clara, CA; George O'Connell, Morris Communication, Augusta, GA; Randall Wright, Wright & Associates, Lake Lotawana, MO

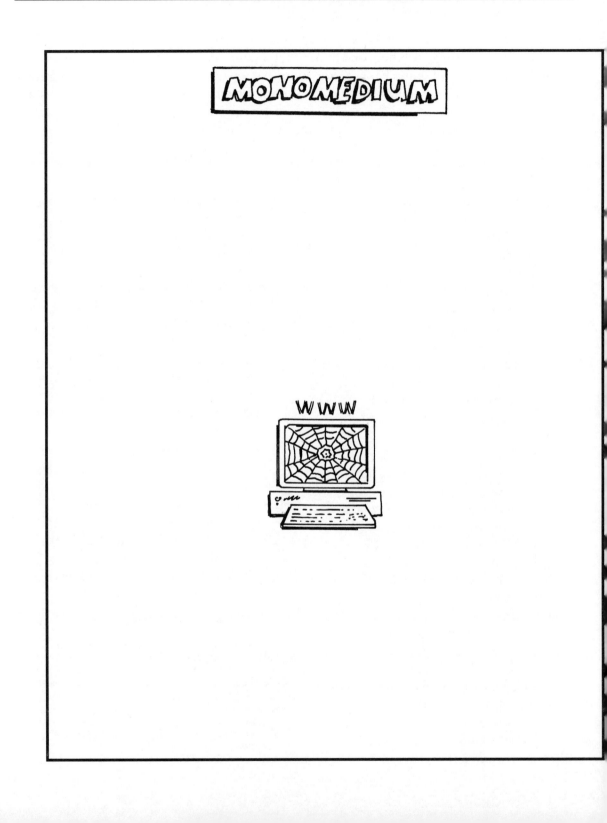

Making Distance Learning SAVI

Learning is best when it is SAVI (Somatic, Auditory, Visual, and Intellectual). Specific learning events can involve two, three, or all of these modes simultaneously. You can check Chapter 5 for more detail on the SAVI approach if you wish. What follows here are a few ideas of what you can do to exercise each of these modes in a CBT (computer-based training) or WBT (Web-based training) environment.

Somatic

Somatic means getting out of your seat and becoming physically active during the learning process. (Clicking a mouse is not physically active.) Too much sitting in front of a computer does the same thing that too much sitting in front of a lecturer does— it dulls the brain. Standing up and moving about improves the body's circulation and, thus, brings fresh energy to the brain.

Here are a few ideas to start you thinking of how you might get people away from the computer screen and up and doing something from time to time.

What follows on the next two pages
are ways to make
distance learning Somatic.

Somatic Learning Ideas

1. **Printout Retrieval.** Have learners print documents from time to time so they have to get up and go to the printer to retrieve them.

2. **Scavenger Hunt.** Have learners go on a scavenger hunt for items and bits of information they can get only by leaving the computer and going to various places in the building.

3. **Pictogram Creation.** Provide learners with colored pens and ask them to create colorful pictograms and learning maps about what they are learning or to complete partially filled-out pictograms with information they retrieve from the computer or other media.

4. **Job-Aid Creation.** Provide colored pens and appropriate templates and craft materials for learners to create their own job aids for use in their work.

5. **Question Cards.** As a review exercise, provide learners with a deck of question cards. Ask them to stand at a table, shuffle the deck, and see which questions they can answer, throwing the cards they can answer into one pile and the ones they can't into another. Then have them review the "can't answer" questions and try again.

6. **Manipulatives.** Provide learners with a box or envelope of objects they can manipulate. This could be a puzzle they have to put together. Or it could be components of a system they have to assemble. Or it could be cards containing the various steps of a process that they have to lay out in the right sequence on a table top or on the floor. Of course, have them get away from the computer and stand when they do this.

7. **Board Game.** As a review of learning, have learners play a board game provided with the course. It could be played on a table top, a magnetic white board, or even on the floor.

8. **Acting Out.** Have learners physically act out a process or procedure– either with objects on a tabletop or with themselves acting as components as they are moving around the room.

9. **Physical Energizer.** Build energy breaks into the program whereby the computer or a separate audio- or videotape can direct learners in a physical exercise of some sort.

10. **Walkman Review.** Provide learners with a Walkman and appropriate audiotapes. At selected times, ask learners to put a specific tape in the Walkman and take a walk. (It's called a Walkman, not a "Sitman"). The tape could contain a concert review of the material just covered on the computer. Or, to help people check their learning, it could contain a series of questions with a pause after each (to allow the learner to answer it) before the correct answer is given.

11. **Personal Interview.** At a certain point in the program, ask learners to leave the computer and interview one or more people in the organization who can provide a brief personal perspective on some aspect of the learning material or answer specific questions. The program could provide a printout of suggested questions to get the conversation going.

12. **Personal Observation.** At a certain point in the program, have the learner leave the computer, go into the office or plant or world and observe something or explore something relative to the subject matter at hand. Then have them record their observations on paper or on the computer, or answer a series of structured questions about their observations.

Auditory

Auditory learners (and we're all auditory learners to one degree or another) learn best when they hear and produce words. The fanciest computer-based training program in the world will never fulfill its potential if it doesn't get learners hearing as well as talking and thinking *out loud* during the learning process. Here are a few ideas about how you might incorporate a strong auditory component into your CBT and WBT programs.

1. **Audio Introduction.** Provide learners with an auditory "learner prep" introduction to the learning program mediated through the computer (if you have the facilities) or through an audiocassette that people can play on a portable tape player or Walkman.

2. **Learner Dialog.** If two people are taking a course together, periodically have them describe out loud to each other what they are learning and how they plan to apply it to their life and work. Or have them ask each other questions to clarify their understanding of the learning material.

3. **Concert Review.** Provide audiotapes containing music together with a verbal review of the concepts, terms, processes, and ideas covered in a specific segment of the training. Try to get learners up on their feet and away from the computer while they do this.

4. **Take-Home Audiotape Review.** Provide audiotapes that people can take with them and listen to in their car stereos or at home while they are doing other things (cooking, getting ready in the morning, walking the dog, etc.).

5. **Auditory Paraphrase.** Ask learners to pause periodically and paraphrase what they have just learned into a tape recorder. After they have created a tape, ask them to play it several times to lock the information into their long-term memory.

6. **Reading Out Loud.** Ask learners to read out loud from computer screens or printed matter in order to add an auditory component to the learning experience.

7. **Question/Answer Audiotape.** To help people check their learning, provide them with an audiotape of questions related to a segment just covered. Each question on the tape would be followed by a pause (to allow the learner to formulate an answer) before the correct answer is given.

8. Interview. Ask learners to leave the computer and interview one or more people in the organization regarding some aspect of what they are learning about. You could provide some suggested questions for them to ask to get them going.

9. Auditory Mnemonics. Create auditory memory devices to help people remember key ideas, terms, or processes. Here are a couple of common examples: *"i before e except after c"* in spelling, and *"righty-tighty, lefty-loosey"* for remembering which way to turn screwdrivers, lightbulbs and jar covers.

10. Thinking Out Loud. Have people perform a function, create a process diagram, build a schematic, or construct a 3-dimensional process model while they talk out loud about everything they are doing and why.

Visual

Visual acuity is strong in everyone. This is because the human mind is more of an image processor than a word processor. Images, because they are concrete, are easy to hang on to. Words, because they are abstract, are much harder to retain. Many CBT and WBT programs are word rich and image poor. By bringing the visual up to at least a parity with the verbal, you can help people learn faster and better. Here are some ideas how.

1. **Course Map.** Provide people with a pictorial map of the course they are taking that gives them "the big picture." They could add to it, color it, laminate it, and keep it as a job aid if they like.

2. **Picture Language.** Use language rich in analogy, metaphor, and imagery to describe concepts, terms, and processes.

3. **Graphics.** Use pictures, diagrams, and other graphics to help make the abstract concrete.

4. **Stories.** Cast parts of the learning material in story form. Stories and concrete examples invoke the image brain of the learner.

5. **Video Examples.** Show learners what you're talking about with video snippets that make everything clear.

6. **Real-World Observations.** Ask learners to leave the computer and observe how something is done inside or outside the office, shop floor, store, or whatever. Then have them type their observations into the computer or write them down on paper in verbal or pictorial form.

7. **Pictogram Creation.** Ask people to create one or more colorful pictograms out of what they are learning. (See Chapter 13 on *Pictograms* in this book.) Their pictograms could be done on normal plain paper or on large flipchart sheets

8. **Pictogram Completion.** Provide people with a partially completed pictogram and ask them to fill in the missing pieces from what they are learning.

9. **Icon Job Aids.** Provide learners with job aids in icon form. Or have learners create their own icon job aids.

10. **Model Creation.** Ask learners to create 3-dimensional models out of what they are learning using objects and craft materials supplied with the course.

11. **Flash Cards.** Ask learners to test their knowledge and understanding of a subject by going through a deck of flash cards.

12. **Peripherals.** Provide people with peripherals in poster or card form containing learning material that they can post around their work space or at home.

13. **Image-Based Concert Review.** While playing music, show a series of PowerPoint-type screens containing images and words that summarize a segment of the learning material just covered.

Intellectual

The word "intellectual" as I'm using it here means involving the mind to create its own learning. Learning is not the storage of information, but the creation of meaning, knowledge, and actionable value by the mind of the learner. Knowledge creation, not information storage, should be one of the major goals of all learning programs. Here are some ideas of what you can do to get the full intellect of the learner involved in learning.

1. **Information Retrieval.** In many cases, it's best to teach people how to access information rather than how to merely store it. The Web is a magnificent information resource for almost any subject. Teaching people how to access information on the Web and translate it into actionable knowledge is a perfect exercise for the learner's intellect.

2. **Problem Solving.** It's often better for a learning program to spend more time posing problems rather than giving answers. Problem solving teaches learners how to think for themselves and how to create meaning, rather than how to mindlessly parrot canned answers.

3. **Conceptual Mapping.** Ask learners to build a coherent conceptual map or flowchart out of what they are learning, combining the various components of a subject together into an integrated whole.

4. **Model Building.** Ask learners to create a 3-dimensional model out of the subject matter that shows how everything fits together to make sense.

5. **Test Making.** As learners listen to an audiotape, watch a video snippet, take a computer-mediated tutorial, or read written material, ask them to create a 10- or 20-question test that they can administer to a partner or colleague taking the same course.

6. **Mental Imagery.** Have learners turn away from the computer, close their eyes, and imagine practicing a skill or having a multisensory experience relative to the learning material. Then have them write down, draw, or describe to another person or a tape recorder, what they experienced. (See Chapter 16 on *Imagery and Learning* for more detail on how to do this.)

7. **Reflection.** Give people time to get away from all media and simply reflect on what they have learned and how they are going to apply it. After a suitable time, ask them to type their reflections into the computer or put them down on paper in verbal and pictorial form.

8. **Question Creation.** Give learners answers and have them them create the questions Jeopardy-style. (See the *Resources* section of this book for inexpensive computerized question games you can incorporate into any technology-driven program.

Making Distance Learning SAVI: A Summary

Somatic (Learning by physical activity)
- Getting away from the computer and moving around
- Field trips
- Using manipulatives (flashcards, models, puzzles)
- Creating something physical
- Physically acting out a process or technology

Auditory (Learning by hearing and talking)
- Describing out loud what you're learning
- Dialoguing with others
- Listening to concert reviews
- Interviewing others
- Creating your own audio reviews

Visual (Learning by seeing)
- Real-world observations
- Reading
- Watching videos
- Creating pictograms
- Making icon job aids

Intellectual (Learning by thinking and imagining)
- Creating mental models
- Reflecting
- Solving problems
- Doing information searches
- Imagining the perfect performance

Some Final Nuggets
Using the Web in the Classroom

You can use the Web in the classroom for individual or team-based learning exercises. Here are just a few ideas to start you thinking.

1. In a sales class, have learners visit competitors' Web sites and share with the class the strengths and weaknesses of the competitors' products, services, or marketing approaches.

2. Have learners use the Web to research and download helpful articles on the subject they are learning about.

3. Create an ongoing message board or chat room for "graduates" of your training program. Have learners use it as a resource in class as well as afterward.

4. Have learners as a class create their own Web-based job aid that they can use as an electronic performance support system on the job.

5. Pose problems for learners to solve in partnerships or small teams that require them to use the Web.

6. Ask graduates of a program to post on an Internet file the most important thing they learned from a program and/or how they are applying the learning on the job. Then have current learners access this file during class and report their findings.

Making Distance Learning Collaborative

Technology can foster social isolation. And learning in isolation has serious limitations for most people, as we all recognize. Therefore it's important to finds ways of using technology to build our community, not destroy. Here are a few ideas of how you might do this.

1. In a video, satellite-based remote classroom setting, follow the 30/70 rule. Make sure that the talking head (or torso) in the studio occupies only 30% or less of the class time and that

70% or more of the time is devoted to partnered and team-based learning exercises. (The role of the facilitator, whether in the classroom or on a remote video screen, is to initiate the learning process and then get out of the way.)

2. Use the same variety of group-based A.L. learning activities in the remote classroom that you'd use in the local one.

3. In a standard Web-based environment, design programs that must be taken by two or more learners together. Build in plenty of occasions for collaborative activities, partnered dialog, and team-based problem-solving exercises– the same ones you would use in an effective classroom setting.

4. If learners must use Web-based programs by themselves, make sure that they are given many opportunities to communicate with others in their immediate environment about the learning material. They can interview others on the job, asking questions, getting information, seeking help. And as part of their learning, when they finish a program they can mentor someone else just starting it.

5. If learners are learning remotely by themselves, assign them one or more cyber-buddies, and build in the necessity for face-to-face, voice-based, and/or e-mail-based dialog with them regarding the learning material and its application to their work.

PART 6

Rapid Instructional Design (RID)

CHAPTER 22

Rapid Design Principles

Rapid Instructional Design (RID)

The need to "do more with less" is not a shallow cliche, but the daily experience of training professionals everywhere. The pressure is on to get better results, and to do it faster.

Scrapping the Traditional ISD Model

Curriculum design in the West over the past 40 years or so has been dominated by the ISD (Instructional Systems Design) model. This model was created in the military during the 2nd World War and has been embellished by a number of training consultants since.

It's still the standard design methodology taught by universities and by most train-the-trainer firms. But it's woefully out-of-date and needs to be scrapped.

Some good, solid thinking has gone into this model. While we want to preserve the best of this thinking, the form in which this thinking has solidified needs to evolve. And the latest research into the brain and learning needs to be acknowledged and incorporated into the process.

Traditional Design Methods

Why the ISD Model No Longer Works

Despite the army of consultants and training companies that still push the ISD model in the training community, more and more people are becoming disillusioned with it. It's just too slow, cumbersome, stiff, linear, and emotionally dull, they say, to really get the job done today. And it's hampered by all sorts of false beliefs about learning.

Rapid Design Methods

The weakness of the ISD model stems in part from its origin–coming out of the military as it did, reflecting a one-sided "male" (i.e., testosterone) point of view almost exclusively, and taking a Behavioristic approach to learning. Its origin explains why it tends to be overly linear, analytical, verbal, "left-brained," academic, top-down, and prescriptive. It seems to have lacked from the start a balancing feminine influence which could have made it more playful, intuitive, image rich, "right-brained," flexible, and emotionally nourishing.

Because of its innate imbalance, the ISD model has often tended to make the design process overly serious, stoical, stressful, wooden, tedious, and slow. And it has been known to often result in lifeless materials, dull presentations, and passive learners.

A superficial tampering with the old ISD model won't work. We need a whole new approach to design — one that proceeds from a new understanding of the learning process, one that is in tune with today's rapid-fire environment, and one that results in better learning and performance for all types of learners.

Why the traditional ISD model should be scrapped

1. It's too time-consuming.

In most cases, we can no longer take six months to design a course. Information gets outdated too quickly for that. Today, course development time needs to be reduced from months to hours. The old rule used to be "20 hours of course design time for every hour of course delivery time." With computer-based instruction, many claim the ratio is more than 150 to 1. Can we really afford this kind of time today?

2. It's overly cognitive, verbal, and rationalistic.

The conventional ISD model trades on the belief that learning is mainly a verbal and cognitive process that must be very linear, very rationalistic, very tidy. Learning certainly involves verbal and cognitive intelligence, but the ISD model fails to give equal time to emotional and intuitive intelligence and the wisdom that comes from all the physical, multisensory, nonlinear, and nonrationalistic modes of learning.

3. It's too top-down and controlling.

The conventional ISD model tends to be hierarchical, paternalistic and prescriptive—a daddy-knows-best kind of thing. Its heavy infusion of Behaviorism tends to make learning rigid and inflexible, emphasizing one right answer and one proper way of doing things. As such, it often treats people as stimulus/response machines who must learn to replicate the perfect performance prescribed by the training program.

4. It tends to treat learners as consumers, not creators.

The ISD model tends to look upon learning as something provided *for* the learner, not something created *by* the learner. It tends to keep learners passive, docile, and dependent as consumers of the learning material provided by the designer. As such, it often neglects to see that *all true learning is that which is created by the learner* through immersion, trial and error, feedback, reflection, and reimmersion.

5. It is often materials-based rather than activity-based.

Much of the time and effort of traditional design goes into the creation of learning materials— PowerPoint presentations, overheads, student workbooks, 3-ring binders, CBT programs, and the rest. The importance of a course is often indicated by the amount and glossiness of the learning materials. Yet, learners learn best by whole-body, contextual, interactive activities, quite apart from the volume and slickness of the materials provided.

Comparing the ISD With the A.L. Approach

Here are some contrasts between an exclusive ISD approach and the approach that many A.L. practitioners prefer to take. This represents tendencies only and is not meant to be a simplistic either/or comparison.

ISD Approach	A.L. Approach
rational	rational-emotive
mind-oriented	mind/body-oriented
mechanistic	natural
rigid & fixed	flexible & open-ended
serious	playful
hierarchical	democratic
individualistic	collaborative
cognitive	multisensory
a one-dish meal	a smorgasbord
presentation driven	activity driven
media-centered	learner-centered
prescriptive	creative
behavioristic	humanistic
left-brained	whole-brained
emphasis on form	emphasis on function

The A.L. Rapid Design Model

Once you evolve out of slavish adherence to the ISD model, transcend some of its more limiting aspects, and extract from it that which is really valuable, you can design effective learning programs much faster.

The ISD model puts a heavy emphasis on instructional media: presentations, materials, computer programs, etc. In contrast, the Rapid Instructional Design (RID) process rids you of much of that. RID proceeds from the belief that people learn more from experience (with feedback) than they do from materials and presentations. You learn how to swim by swimming, how to sell by selling, and how to manage by managing. You don't learn any new skill by merely listening to someone talk about it, whether an instructor, a book, or a computer.

Yet, the biggest bulk of time in traditional design is spent in creating materials and presentations (i.e., information-shoveling devices). Yet this has the least impact on learning. By ridding yourself of having to design elaborate learning materials, and designing learning experiences instead, you can save a mountain of time while getting far better results. You do less. Learners do more. Everybody wins.

Many A.L. designers have RID themselves of materials-heavy and presentation-heavy courses that took many months to develop and have replaced them with activity-based courses that they have designed in hours. Most often this has resulted in reduced training time, a higher level of learner involvement, and much better learning.

Activity-Centered Training

Training that is activity-centered rather than media-centered has proven superior again and again. It puts learners squarely in charge of their own learning and enables them to learn with and from each other. "Knowledge is experience," said Einstein. "Everything else is just information."

The designer's role, then, is to provide a lively context in which learners can work with each other to create their own content (i.e., meaning, knowledge, skill, value). The guiding principle is: Never do for learners what learners can do for themselves and for each other. Rapid Instructional Design works because it never attempts to do everything for the learner or totally control the learning process. Rather, it makes learners the responsible agents of their own learning.

People learn more from real life experience (with feedback) than they learn from presentations and materials, no matter how sophisticated, polished, and "creative" they might be.

Designing Learning Experiences

When you are designing learner-centered activities, ask yourself, "What do people actually have to do and be on the job to be successful?" Figure out what that is and then have learners do exactly that through a series of experiences— moving from simple to complex. Each experience can be followed by feedback, reflection, and retrial as appropriate.

You really don't need lots of tricks, clever gimmicks, "creative techniques," and shallow hoopla. That often just gets in the way and gives you the illusion of learning when no real learning is taking place and no lasting value is being created. What you really need is learner activities that allow learners to work with each other in as "real world" a setting as possible to create their own personal meaning, knowledge, and skill.

The 7 Principles of Rapid Design

Following these seven simple, natural principles will enable you to speed the design process while developing more effective learning programs. The 7 Principles are:

1. Design with the 4-Phase Learning Cycle.

2. Appeal to all learning styles.

3. Make your designs activity-based.

4. Create a learning community.

5. Alternate between physically active and physically passive learning activities.

6. Follow the 30/70 rule.

7. Create a flexible, open-ended design.

Here's a little more detail on each:

1. Design with the 4-Phase Learning Cycle.

The Rapid Instructional Design model is built on the 4 phases of the human learning process:

1. Preparation (arousal)

2. Presentation (encounter)

3. Practice (integration)

4. Performance (application)

All 4 phases must be present and in proper balance for true learning to occur.

It is common for designs to emphasize Phase 2 while glossing over Phases 1, 3, and 4. ("We haven't got time for all that. Just give them the information.") In fact, we often put 80% or more of our time, energy, and money into creating Phase 2 stuff: presentations, materials, manuals, computer programs, etc. Yet Phase 2 contributes, at best, probably only 20% to the actual learning. Phases 1, 3, and 4 are far more crucial. It is what the learner says and does that is more important for the actual learning than what the media (presenter, manual, computer program) says and does.

Before you design, review chapters 6-10 in this book on the 4-phase cycle of learning. It will help you achieve a strong, balanced structure that will result in better learning every time.

2. Appeal to all learning styles.

Everyone learns best in an option-rich environment that appeals to all learning styles and sensory modes. Make your learning designs **SAVI** (Somatic, Auditory, Visual, and Intellectual), and it will improve everyone's learning.

Somatic involves physical activity during the learning process. Sitting too much, whether in a classroom or behind a computer, can be draining. Standing, moving about, and doing something physical from time to time gets the whole body involved, improves circulation to the brain, and enhances learning.

Auditory involves *learners* talking out loud about what they are learning. It is often true, as Sharon Bowman points out in her book *Presenting with Pizzaz*, that the person doing the most talking is doing the most learning. When learners talk out loud about what they're learning it stimulates the sensory and motor cortices (and other areas of the brain) to solidify and integrate the learning.

Visual involves seeing, creating, and integrating images of all kinds. Visual communication is more powerful than verbal communication for the simple reason that human beings have more equipment in their heads for processing visual information than for any other sense. What you **see** (rather than what you hear others saying in endless words) is what you **get**.

Intellectual involves using the mind itself (with no other input from the senses) to reflect on experience and create meaning. After you have used all your senses to take in an experience, it's the mind that translates this into meaning. The mind is "auto-didactic," a fancy word that means the mind teaches itself through reflection and problem solving, and by creating mental models (actually new neural networks) out of what it has experienced.

Of course, different people prefer different mixes of these four SAVI elements, but engaging in all four has proven to enhance learning for all learners.

3. Make your designs activity-based.

People learn far more from active experiences than they'll ever learn from presentations and materials, no matter how technologically sophisticated those presentations and materials might be.

So when designing a new learning program, don't ask first off what materials and presentations you'll have to produce. Ask first off what *activities* people can engage in that will help them pick up the new knowledge and skill quickly.

You will need some materials, some presentations, and some media most likely. But these should be minimal and a supplement to the active learning process and not a substitute for it. You can RID yourself of more useless baggage than you realize, and end up with a tighter design, happier learners, and a much more satisfying long-range result.

There is evidence scattered throughout this book showing how and why this is true.

4. Create a learning community.

The excessive individualism of Western culture when applied to education has had a negative effect on real learning (learning as the creation of new meaning, knowledge, skill, and value). All good learning has a social base to it. We know this as children. We forget this as adults.

There is literally tons of research indicating that peer teaching is superior to any other form of instruction.

That's why it is so strange that we persist in creating learning programs for isolated individuals rather than for communities of learners.

Linking is the essence of intelligence, whether between neurons in the brain or learners in a learning community. The more interconnectivity there is, the more intelligence there is. Excessive individualism disconnects people from community and dumbs everyone down.

As much as possible, create designs that allow everyone in a learning community to be both a learner and a teacher simultaneously. When people take a measure of responsibility for each other's learning success, everyone benefits.

5. Alternate between physically active and physically passive learning activities.

Traditional learning designs tend to keep people physically passive most of the time. Glazing and learning ineffectiveness often result. When the body falls asleep, the mind does too. But getting people up periodically to do something physical helps keep the body and mind alert.

A physical activity can take many forms: standing and talking, manipulating physical objects, acting out processes, creating models or pictograms, putting on demonstrations, or engaging in a hands-on activity of some sort.

A physically passive learning activity generally takes place when people are sitting down and doing things like observing, thinking, reflecting, building mental models, listening to presentations, interacting with computers, and the like.

When designing the active portions of a learning program ask yourself: "If people could not sit still for more than 20 minutes at a time, what could I have them do that would help them master the learning material?"

Studies have shown that getting up, moving about, and doing something physical from time to time improves circulation to the brain. And when brain circulation improves, so does learning.

Designs are best when they do not keep people either physically passive or physically active for long stretches of time, but alternate between the two continually. The constant back- and-forth rhythm between the physically active and the physically passive modes tends to sustain people's energy and improve their learning.

6. Follow the 30/70 rule.

Don't take this as a dogmatic absolute, but it's often best to devote 30% (or less) of learning time to instructor or media presentations and 70% (or more) to learner practice and integration activities.

This ratio can differ, of course, depending on the subject matter and the audience, but it's a good guideline to keep in mind.

Often the ratio is reversed, with the presentation (be it from an instructor, a computer program, or whatever) consuming the bulk of the time. Very little is learned and job transference suffers as a result.

A good design gets the ball in the learner's court as often and for as long as possible. This is because it is what the learner says and does that is more important for the actual learning than what the instructor or instructional media says and does.

You don't learn to play tennis by watching your instructor hit the ball, but by hitting the ball yourself. It's as simple as that.

Traditional design tends to treat learners as consumers of presentations and learning materials. Accelerated learning design tends to treat learners as creators of their own knowledge, meaning, and skill.

Learning, after all, is not a spectator sport, but a highly participative one. And teaching is not a performing art but a matter of orchestrating a learning environment to get learners totally involved in their own learning.

7. Create a flexible, open-ended design.

Learning programs designed with the traditional ISD model have tended to be rigid, prescriptive, inflexible, and set in cement. Often they have been designed to be replicated over and over again in exactly the same way. Packaged programs are sometimes like that. So are computer-based training and Web-based training programs. And their inflexible nature tends to make them difficult to modify.

The problem is that in today's world, nothing stays the same for very long, and rigid one-size-fits-all programs are quickly outmoded.

By contrast, accelerated learning design seeks to be open-ended and responsive to change. It seeks to create flexible learning programs that are always "works in progress" and that are intended to continually evolve and improve.

It takes considerable pressure off designers when they realize that they don't have to design a once-and-for-all, perfect, set-in-cement learning program, but one that has built within it the seeds of its own constant evolution.

A traditional, heavily prescriptive program is like a plastic plant. It always remains the same. An accelerated learning program, by contrast, is like a live plant, always establishing new roots, putting our new shoots, opening new sprouts, always growing.

Any program you design can keep growing naturally as you solicit ideas from the learners themselves about how to improve it and keep it evolving. It helps to think of the learning community not only as coteachers, but as codesigners as well.

CHAPTER 23

The 7-Step
Rapid Design Process

1. **Determine desired goals and outcomes.**

2. **Plan the main dish.**
   (The Presentation and Practice Phases)

3. **Plan the appetizers.**
   (The Preparation Phase)

4. **Plan the dessert.**
   (The Performance Phase)

5. **Cook the food.**
   (Sequence Steps 2-4 and develop materials)

6. **Serve the meal.**
   (Deliver the course)

7. **Improve the meal.**
   (Evaluate and enhance the learning experience)

Rapid Design Process Overview

1. **Determine desired goals and outcomes.**

   What values does this program intend to create?

   What tasks do people have to perform to create these values?

   What knowledge, skills, and attitudes will people need in order to perform these tasks successfully?

2. **Plan the main dish. (The Presentation/Practice Phases)**

    What experiences, activities, and exercises will best help people achieve the goals of this learning program?

    How will I get learners totally involved in their own learning?

    How will I appeal to all learning styles and sensory modes (SAVI)?

    If presentations are necessary, how can I get learners to participate in them actively and creatively?

    How will I get learners to work together to help each other learn?

3. **Plan the appetizers. (The Preparation Phase)**

    What learner benefits will I stress?

    How will I create a positive *physical* environment?
    • Ideas for peripherals, room arrangement, music, decorations, etc.

    How will I create a positive *social* environment?
    • Ideas for creating a learning community right from the start.

    How will I create a positive *emotional* environment?
    • What positive suggestions will I make?
    • How will I remove barriers and instill optimism in learners?

    Will I have a theme? If so, what?

    How might I help prepare learners before they show up?

4. **Plan the dessert. (The Performance Phase)**

    How can people reinforce and apply their new learning *at* the session?

    How can people reinforce, apply, and extend their new learning *after* the session?

How can I get learners to help improve the learning program?

What structural support will help reinforce the new learning on the job?

5. Cook the food. (Refine and sequence Steps 2-4 and gather materials.)

Decide on your "final" starting design.

Evaluate and refine your structure.

Develop and gather the materials you will need.

6. Serve the meal.

Deliver the program.

7. Improve the meal.

What's working well and should be retained?

What needs to be dropped, added, or enhanced?

How can even our goals be sharpened and refined?

Modify Steps 1-6 accordingly.

**What follows is another level of detail
on each of these steps.**

Determine Desired Goals and Outcomes

It was common years ago for companies to spend months doing a front-end needs analysis before designing a training program. No more. Increasingly, we are forced to deal with short time frames for training design. What used to be, "We need it next year!" is becoming, "We need it next Thursday!"

Today, if we took six months to do a needs analysis, by the time we got our data together, it would be out-dated. So we must determine goals and outcomes quickly and be ready to continually refine those goals and outcomes throughout the life of a program.

Here's a step-by-step process you can follow to get your goals together quickly.

1. Talk to a few key people from a number of levels and departments within an organization who are stakeholders in the training program. Ask managers, rank-and-file workers, customers, potential participants, etc., this question: "From your perspective, what do we need?" Make a quick composite of what they tell you.

2. Revisit these same people with your composite and have them give you their feedback and reactions to it.

3. With the refined composite in mind, use your intuition as well as your reason to answer these questions out loud with one or more others, recording your responses quickly with words, pictures, or on audiotape.

    -   What end results, accomplishments, and values does this program need to create?

    -   What tasks do people have to perform in order to produce these results, accomplishments, and values?

    -   What attitudes, skills, and knowledge will help people perform these tasks successfully?

    -   How will we determine how well the goals have been achieved?

4. Put #3 into a verbal (and pictorial?) summary of a page or less.

5. Check back with your stakeholders to get their reactions to your summary of program goals.

6. After the program is up and running, revisit and fine-tune your goals continually, based on the experience you are having with the program.

Plan the Main Dish (The Presentation / Practice Phases)

This is the tennis court of learning. Following the 30/70 rule, try to get the ball in the learners' court 70% of the time or more. Here are some step-by-step questions to answer that will help you plan your main dish quickly.

- Start by asking: "What activities might the learners engage in that will get them thoroughly involved in the learning?" Only then ask: "What presentations and materials will I need to support these activities?"

- When presentations are made, how will I keep learners creatively involved?

- How will I assure that the learning is fully SAVI?

- How will I assure that the ball stays in the learners' court at least 70% of the time?

- How will I assure a balanced mix of physically active and physically passive learning activities for this program?

- Will I use a theme? If so, what and how?

- What are the many ways that I can get learners to collaborate to help each other learn?

Here are some additional suggestions:

1. Don't be at all concerned with sequencing at this point in the design process. Just collect as many ideas as you can randomly.

2. If possible, have one or more other people work on this with you— out loud.

3. As you talk, capture your ideas on tape, or on individual cards (that can be sorted later), or on a large wall or table mural using words, pictures, and color. Use any means that works best for you for capturing the main ingredients of the Presentation and Performance Phases.

4. Show your results to others for their comments and suggestions.

5. Let this simmer in the pot while you go on to the next phases.

Plan the Appetizers (The Preparation Phase)

Getting people open and ready to learn is the essential first step in learning. What the Preparation Phase seeks to accomplish is to give people a relationship with the subject that's positive. It is the *relationship* between the learner and the subject matter that determines the quality and quantity of learning that will go on. A negative relationship slows learning (or stops it altogether). A positive relationship accelerates and deepens the learning.

You can help learners create a positive relationship with the subject matter by:

- Making positive suggestions
- Having clear, meaningful goals
- Clarifying for learners the benefits of the learning
- Raising learners' curiosity
- Providing a relaxed and stimulating environment
- Getting learners out of isolation and into community
- Humanizing the experience

Before a Program Starts

Here are some questions to answer to determine what you can do prior to a learning program to prepare people for a positive learning experience.

- Will I have a learner prep kit?

- If so, what will it contain?

- What positive suggestions will I make?

- What learner benefits will I highlight?

- How can I state the learning goals in an appealing way?

- Will I use e-mail to create interest? How?

- Will I use personal or phone contact? How?

- What are all the other ways I can think of for preparing people for an optimal learning experience ahead of time?

When a Program Starts

Here are some questions to answer to determine what you can do at the start of a program to help prepare learners for a positive learning experience.

- How can I state the learning goals in an appealing way?

- How will I present the learner benefits?

- What positive suggestions can I make?

- What will I do to assure a positive physical environment?
  - seating arrangement
  - peripherals
  - music
  - room decorations

- How will I create a learning community from the start?

- How will I get people active and learning right off the bat?

- If I use a theme, how will I relate it to the subject matter?

Plan the Dessert (The Performance Phase)

We hear so often that some training programs have poor transference to the job. There are perhaps many reasons for this; some not having to do with training at all. But one training-related reason might be that there has not been a strong Phase 4 built into the program design. And without a strong Phase 4, the 4-Phase Cycle is incomplete and the long-term effectiveness of the training program deteriorates.

The Performance Phase has two parts: What learners do at the end of a program and what they do after the program.

At the End of a Learning Program

Here are some questions you can ask yourself when designing the in-program portion of the Performance Phase.

- How can learners "put it all together" and demonstrate that they have integrated the knowledge or the skill?

- What can learners do at the session to plan for their application of their new knowledge or skill to the job?

- What can learners do at the session to help improve the effectiveness of the learning program itself?

After a Learning Program

Here are some questions you can ask yourself when designing the on-the-job, follow-through portion of the Performance Phase.

- How can we assure that the learners will apply and extend their learning on the job?

- What additional supports and reinforcements will we provide?

- What can we put in place to enable learners to help each other achieve higher performance and greater value?

- What organizational blocks may hamper good performance? How can we eliminate, reduce, or get around these?

- How will we go about learning from graduates on the job how to strengthen and enhance the learning program?

Cook the Food

Now is the time to put the result of the first four steps together into a coherent and unified program and to develop any materials you might need (agendas, learning aids, exercises, peripherals, job aids, etc.)

It is at this point, and only this point, that you begin sequencing the various elements of the program. When sequencing the results of Step 2 (the Presentation and Practice Phases) it's good to keep the following in mind:

- Remember the 30/70 rule— 30% of class time for facilitator presentations and 70% for learner practice activities.

- Remember to alternate between physically active and physically passive learning activities throughout the program.

- Remember to include the full range of SAVI learning techniques in as many of the activities as you can.

- Remember the simple rule: Never do for learners what learners can do for themselves and for each other.

- Foster lots of collaboration among learners whenever you can.

- Resist the temptation to overdesign and overstructure, but keep the learning program flexible, open, and responsive to the immediate needs of the learners.

Serve the Meal

The menu has been planned. The food has been cooked. The table is set. Now let everyone enjoy a nourishing meal. Some learners, however, may have "eating disorders" based on earlier learning experiences. They may have been force-fed or given the wrong kind of nourishment. (There is a lot of junk food out there in the training world as you know. Some of it takes the form of highly scripted, linear, hierarchal, and mechanistic learning programs. And some of it takes the form of fluff, hoopla, and so called "creative" techniques that may be clever and entertaining but produce no deep nourishment and no long-term value.)

Let your learning program be different. Don't allow it to be educational junk food but to be something substantial that involves learners on a deeper level and is results-driven through and through. If you facilitate your learning program according to A.L. principles, it should result in a nourishing experience for the learners that produces strong lasting value. The key is to stay flexible and open, remembering that the learners themselves, and not your media and methods, are the most important component of the learning program. As Jacques Barzun put it in his book *Begin Here:* "Teaching is not the application of a system. It is an exercise in perpetual discretion."

Learning programs that seem to always produce the greatest value are flexible, learner-centered, collaborative, option-rich, enjoyable, challenging, and SAVI.

When you are a learning facilitator, remember:

- The facilitator's role is to initiate the learning process and then get out of the way.

- "Stand and Deliver" is a very outmoded image of a facilitator's role.

- The facilitator is there not to perform in front of the learners but to create a context in which the learners can work with each other to create meaningful learning.

Improve The Meal
(Evaluate and Enhance the Learning Experience)

Evaluation of the learning and of the learning program itself should be a normal part of every program. The reason for evaluation is to constantly improve the learning program so that it can constantly improve the learning.

You should treat every run of a learning program as a pilot. The learning program is never set in cement, but is forever evolving and forever being enhanced. Another way of saying this is that the design of the program is never finished but is a constant work in process.

Evaluating the Learning Program

Level 1 evaluations (smile sheets) can tell you something about a learner's reaction to a program, but they can't be fully trusted as a true measure of learning. A study by IBM in the 80s indicated that the people who were evaluating a learning program with 7s and 8s (on a scale of 10) were, on average, more successful in applying the learning on the job than those who gave the program 9s and 10s. Hmm.

If you are going to use student evaluations, are there ways you can humanize the process and make it a stronger tool for enhancing the learning program?

One way is to put people in teams and give them five minutes or so to come up with three or more creative ideas for enhancing the program and the learning experience. The learners, then, who are now your codesigners will deliver to you a wealth of ideas that you can use immediately for enhancing the training program. You will be astonished at how many good, usable ideas they come up with.

Another idea is to interview graduates of a program several weeks afterward and ask them questions like: "Now that you're on the job, what helped you the most in the learning program?"; "What helped you the least?"; "What would you like to have seen more of in the program?"; "Less of?"; "Now that you're doing the work, what more do you need that could help you be more successful?"

The information gathered from in-class and post-class evaluations can be used to modify and enhance all aspects of the learning program on a continuing basis.

Other Evaluations of a Program's Success

Level 2 evaluation tests the immediate recall of information or performance of a skill. This will give you some good information, but it can't be fully trusted either. Sometimes people who test well will fall apart on the job. And sometimes people with test anxiety who don't do so well on the test will end up being high performers on the job.

Level 3 evaluation measures job performance. It would be well if your design could have built into it some criteria for doing a Level 3. The data that result from this type of evaluation are perhaps a better evaluation of the learning than Level 2, since it tests long-term transference of the learning.

Level 4 evaluation (the "So What" indicator) seeks to get at the value and benefit to the organization's business, culture, customers, etc., that the learning program has brought. This sometimes is the hardest information to get at, but it is the most valuable when determining the success of a program.

PART 7

The Learning Revolution and You

CHAPTER 24

The Soul of an A.L. Practitioner

How to Achieve Success With A.L.

Becoming a successful A.L. practitioner is not a mechanical skill that you can acquire without the full participation of your whole self. This is because A.L. is not just one more set of clever, creative, fluffy techniques that you can smear on your old assumptions about learning, but a whole new set of assumptions. The important point is this: A.L. is systemic, not cosmetic. It's a *philosophy* that departs from conventional notions of learning in some significant ways. And it requires certain qualities of heart, mind, and soul if you are to achieve the greatest amount of success with it. Your whole being has to resonate with the A.L. philosophy, and you have to sense its human implications on a deep level, or everything you do with A.L. will be slightly out of tune, disjointed, shallow, uninspired, and (in terms of long-range value) ineffective.

The 3 Cs of the Successful A.L. Facilitator

The qualities in you that are most likely to help make you successful with A.L. are your **Care, Creativity,** and **Courage.** A word about each.

Care

To be successful with A.L., it's essential that you care for people and care for the subject matter you're dealing with.

Care for People. Genuine care for people will take you a long way in achieving success as an A.L. practitioner. Being a learning facilitator is a form of love. It's a way to help other human beings find and create value for themselves. It's a way of awakening people to new potentials and possibilities within

> The exercise of care, creativity, and courage is essential if you are to have the maximum success with A.L.

themselves and within the world. It's a way to help people achieve a larger measure of awakeness, success, satisfaction, and joy in their work and in their lives.

An A.L. practitioner is not primarily an information conduit, but a nurturer. He or she is not interested primarily in rigidly applying a given learning system to everyone in the same way, but is flexible and responsive to each learner's unique set of perceptions, talents, and learning abilities. The aim is not to create a mechanically repeatable and successful learning "system," but to create successful learners, no matter what system or systems are used or what rigid rules and principles have to be bent.

Care for people requires that you not try to be central to learners or make them dependent on you but that you know when to get out of their way. Good learning facilitators are like good parents. They work for their own obsolescence. And they are successful to the degree that they can disappear, like a first-stage rocket, while the payload they boost soars way beyond them.

Care for Your Subject. If your care for people is primary, care for your subject follows close behind. Subjects taught in a mechanical, perfunctory, emotionless way tend to fall flat for the learner. Genuine interest in your subject, even passion for it, is essential if you want to have a maximum impact on your learners. If a subject you are teaching doesn't turn you on, how can you expect learners to get excited about it?

Passion! How absent this is from so many learning environments! And how essential it is for accelerated learning! Books about training and train-the-trainer programs tend to emphasize the trainer's use of methods, techniques, and media and tend to overlook the one thing needful— the trainer's passion for the subject. Any learning program becomes shallow and ineffective when it's all technique and no heart. It's the heart, the soul, the passion of the facilitator that learners really pick up on more than the methods, techniques, and media being used.

Of course, genuine care for a subject is not enough. It must be coupled with good accelerated learning approaches and

I don't know what your destiny will be, but one thing I do know: The only ones among you who will be really happy are those who have sought and found how to serve.

—Albert Schweitzer

techniques if optimal learning and performance outcomes are to be achieved. But without that care, that interest, and that passion, learning can't even get off the ground.

Creativity

"Teaching is not the application of a system; it's an act of perpetual discretion," says Jacques Barzun. I would add that it's also an act of perpetual creation.

As this book repeatedly points out, there's a massive need for a revolution in learning in our culture today. All of us in the learning field are being called upon not to mindlessly and soullessly repeat the past but to mindfully and soulfully invent the future.

A.L.'s rallying cry is "Innovate! Innovate! Innovate!" And it's not a matter of innovating for innovation's sake, but for the sake of awakening people to their full potential for learning and for life.

Of course, many of us live and work in organizations that tend to subvert this, to stifle creativity either some of the time or most of the time. But we can't let that stop us. To be a responsible learning professional today means to exercise creativity, despite any temporary inhibitors in the environment. To be a responsible learning professional today means to creatively lead the way.

Courage

It takes a certain amount of guts to be a learning leader today, to exert your creativity and to break out of the grey, inhibiting confines of establishment assumptions about learning. Courage does not mean having an arrogant or dogmatically prescriptive attitude about learning, but being willing to try new things, to risk failure, to "wobble," to depart from the norm, to be open to new understanding, to dare to be everything you essentially are, and to constantly be ready to learn. Without courage, you're dead meat— just one more lifeless robot in an

> Be the change you want to see in the world.
>
> –Ghandi

unconscious civilization. But with courage you can be a positive influence in your organization, awakening yourself and others to the endless possibilities of life.

Page Smith, the founding provost of the University of California at Santa Cruz, says that true education, an education designed to produce a true person, must include instruction in courage. In his book about the foibles of higher education called *Killing the Spirit*, he writes this:

> "Great things are not accomplished by cowards but always by individuals bold enough— or perhaps in some situations, mad enough— to fly in the face of the most firmly held and respected conventions of their society."

It is courage that leads, courage that forms new cultures, courage that helps keep individuals and organizations and societies healthy. Without courage, we cannot create. And without creativity, we cannot properly educate and care for ourselves or others.

Care, Creativity, and Courage. Each is like a leg on a three-legged stool. When any one leg is missing, the whole thing collapses. But when all three legs are intact, it gives us something solid to stand on as learning facilitators and lifts us to a higher perspective.

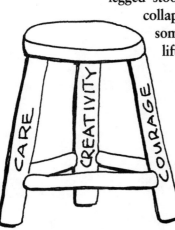

CHAPTER 25

Growing A.L. in Your Organization

Accelerated Learning is much more than a collection of creative learning ideas and techniques. It is a whole, integrated philosophy and approach to learning that stands in contrast to many of our conventional beliefs and practices. It is systemic, not cosmetic, and requires a shift in some of our basic assumptions about learning if it is to be truly successful in an organization.

Therefore, in order to grow A.L. in your organization, A.L. needs to infiltrate that organization and its people on many levels simultaneously.

You know how true that is. You can have the best ideas in the world, but nonsupportive management, antiquated beliefs about learning, and structures that are antithetical to fresh, creative ideas can kill them almost before they are born.

Your organization is a living organism. As an organism, it can have structures that are learning disabled, learning disabling, and self-limiting. It can have cultural habits that keep it (and the people in it) from constantly learning, growing, and evolving. So if you want to create a learning revolution where you work, you've got to deal with your organization as a whole and let A.L. beliefs and practices touch it on many levels.

Here is just a starter set of suggestions of what you might do to support the learning revolution and help make your organization a healthier place in which to live and work.

Success in changing the educational infrastructure in your organization will not come from implementing just one or two of these suggestions, but many of them

simultaneously— and continually. Check those suggestions that you can most easily implement today and in the months ahead that you feel will have the greatest impact.

Ideas for Multidimensional Growth

1. Get a critical mass of your organization's training professionals trained in accelerated learning philosophies and techniques.

2. Educate management through seminars, mini-workshops, presentations, and one-on-one conversations.

3. Get A.L. on the agenda of departmental meetings and management pow-wows.

4. Schedule periodic gatherings for A.L. practitioners where they can exhibit their wares, do show-and-tells, and solicit fresh ideas from each other.

5. Set A.L. standards for all course development, whether classroom-based or technology-driven.

6. Set A.L. standards for the evaluation of facilitators.

7. Ask managers of all levels to brainstorm with A.L. practitioners on ways to improve learning throughout the organization.

8. Recognize staff members who are making innovative contributions to accelerated, enhanced learning in your organization and reward them appropriately.

9. Stop worshiping the company culture. Don't be insensitive, but just go ahead and improve learning wherever you can without waiting for permission or following convention.

10. Draw up a three-year plan for bringing Accelerated Learning to your organization. Get top management to sign off on it.

11. Make improving learning throughout the organization an essential part of each manager's responsibility.

12. Transform a key course into an Accelerated Learning format. Measure the before and after. Get the numbers. Verify the

---

After a time of decay comes the turning point. The powerful light that has been banished returns. There is movement, but it is not brought about by force. The movement is natural, arising spontaneously. For this reason the transformation of the old becomes easy. The old is discarded and the new is introduced. Both measures accord with the time; therefore no harm results.

—I Ching

improved ROI (return on investment). Repeatedly advertise this improvement to management and everyone else in the organization.

13. Create and circulate a periodic camcorded video featuring successful A.L. applications. It can include show-and-tells, interviews, and scenes of classes in action.

14. Train masses of people in your organization in how to do one-on-one OJT (on-the job training) using accelerated learning techniques.

15. Hold breakfast or brown-bag meetings open to all employees on how to learn faster and better, together with tips for helping their children do the same.

16 In place of (or in addition to) normal evaluations, have learners in teams brainstorm ways of accelerating and enhancing a learning program they have just experienced.

17 Display in a prominent place an exhibit of A.L. memorabilia: principles, successes, pictures, materials, techniques, resources, ideas, etc.

18. Scatter accelerated learning tips and ideas in small, colorful peripherals (posters, mobiles, job aids, etc.) around the office — by the snack machine, next to wall clocks, in elevators and hallways, in rest rooms, in classrooms, on desks, on cafeteria tables, on the floor— wherever people are likely to see them.

19. Invite graduates of an A.L.-based program to share their experiences (and results) with people just embarking on the same program.

20. Distribute short audiotapes with tips and techniques for learning in an accelerated mode.

21. Invite top brass and mid-managers to sit in on classes in which participants are discussing how A.L. approaches are helping their learning and their performance.

23. Have a learning fair for the organization with booths and presentations for A.L. practitioners to show their wares and share their experiences.

Staying alive, whether as an individual or an organization, requires remaining open to the process of continual innovation, transformation, and renewal.

24. Get the local press and trade magazines to publish stories on your learning successes.

25. Make presentations on your successes at local and national meetings of trainers that attract people from your organization.

26. Sponsor periodic get-togethers (for a day or half day) of A.L. practitioners from all organizations in your community who want to share their successes and help each other with their challenges.

27. Send people periodic e-mail reminders and tips on how to accelerate and enhance their learning.

28. Create an Internet depository of A.L. tips and techniques that all learning facilitators can tap into for ideas. Have everyone contribute to its growth.

29. Publish a periodic review of A.L successes in both print and Internet format.

30. Provide an A.L.-type program for your organization's clients that shows them how to use your products and services most effectively.

A.L. Strategic Planning

In strategizing with others about how to grow A.L. in your organization and when developing both short-term and long-term strategic plans, here are some questions you can ask:

- What positive energies exist that support the A.L. approach? How can we optimize these?

- What benefits can A.L. bring to the organization economically, culturally, and humanly?

- What people can we link together to begin to build a networked infrastructure to strengthen A.L. approaches in the organization?

- What management support currently exists that should be nourished? How might we do this?

> In the main, the bureaucratic structure of the workplace is more powerful in determining what professionals do than are personal abilities, professional training, or previous experience. Therefore, efforts should focus on changing the structure of the workplace, not on changing the teachers.
>
> –Jack Frymier
> *Phi Delta Kappan*

- What structures, beliefs, assumptions, practices, cultural habits, and barriers are currently inhibiting the growth of learning and creativity in the organization? How can we remove, reduce, isolate, or get around these?

- How can we best demonstrate a powerful ROI (return on investment) with A.L. that will generate continuing and additional management support?

Learning Our Way Into a Positive Future

The future belongs to the learners. Only those organizations and individuals who can continually learn will survive and thrive. And the learning that will bring the brightest future is learning that concentrates not merely on how to make money but how to work and live in a way that honors our humanity; ignites the full range of all our intelligences; and respects, nurtures, and preserves the earth.

Come to the edge, he said. They said, We are afraid. Come to the edge, he said. They came. He pushed them... and they flew.
—Guillaume Apollinaire

RESOURCES

Literature, Music, Organizations

THE BRAIN AND LEARNING

Caine, Renate Nummela and Geoffrey Caine. *Making Connections: Teaching and the Human Brain,* Addison-Wesley, 1994.

Caine, Renate Nummela and Geoffrey Caine. *Unleashing the Power of Perpetual Change: The Potential of Brain-Based Teaching,* ASCD, 1997.

Diamond, Marian. *Enriching Heredity: The Impact of the Environment on the Brain,* Free Press, 1988.

Diamond, Marian. *Magic Trees of the Mind,* E.P. Dutton, 1998.

Golden, Daniel. "Building a Better Brain," *National Geographic,* June 1994.

Hart, Leslie. *Human Brain and Human Learning,* Longman Publishing, 1983.

Herrmann, Ned. *The Creative Brain,* Ned Herrmann Group, 1995.

Jensen, Eric. *Brain Based Learning,* Turning Point Publishing, 1996.

Jensen, Eric. *Introduction to Brain-Compatible Learning,* The Brain Store, 1988.

Jensen, Eric. *Teaching With the Brain in Mind,* ASCD, 1998.

LeDoux, Joseph. *The Emotional Brain,* Simon & Schuster, 1996.

Russell, Peter. *The Brain Book,* Plume, 1979.

Short, Cynthia. *Dendrites Are Forever* (workbook with exercises for maintaining and growing brain capacity into old age), self-published (406) 862-1095.

Sylwester, Robert. *A Celebration of Neurons: An Educator's Guide to the Human Brain,* ASCD, 1995.

THE MIND-BODY CONNECTION

Brink, Susan. "Smart Moves– New Research Suggests That Folks From 8 to 80 Can Shape Up Their Brains With Aerobic Exercise," *US News and World Report,* May 15, 1995, pp. 78-82.

Dennison, Paul and Gail. *Brain Gym, Teachers Edition,* Edu-Kinesthetics, 1994.

Hannaford, Carla. *Smart Moves: Why Learning Is Not All in Your Head,* Great Ocean Publishers, 1995.

Hannaford, Carla, Cherokee Shaner, Sandry Zachary, and Linda Grinde. *Education in Motion,* Edible Elephant Publications, 1991.

Pert, Candice. *Molecules of Emotion: The Science Behind Mind-Body Medicine*, Simon & Schuster, 1997 & 1999.

Primislow, Sharon. *Making the Brain-Body Connection*, Kinetic Publishing, 1998.

Spretnak, Charlene. *The Resurgence of the Real: Body, Nature, and Place in a Hypermodern World*, Routledge, 1999.

GENERAL REFERENCES ON ACCELERATED LEARNING

DePorter, Bobbi. *Quantum Learning*, Dell, 1992.

Dryden, Gordon and Jeannette Vos. *The Learning Revolution: To Change the Way the World Learns*, The Learning Web, 1994 & 1999.

Fairbanks, Deborah. *Accelerated Learning*, ASTD Infoline (issue 9209).

Frischnecht, Jacqueline and Glen Capelli. *Maximizing Your Learning Potential*, Kendall/Hunt, 1995.

Gill, Mary Jane and David Meier. "Accelerated Learning Takes Off at Bell Atlantic," *Training & Development Journal,* ASTD, January 1989.

Linksman, Ricki. *How to Learn Anything Quickly: An Accelerated Learning Program for Rapid Learning*, Citadel Press, 1996.

Lozanov, Georgi. *Suggestology and Outlines of Suggestopedia*, Gordon and Breach, 1978.

Ostrander, Nancy, Shiela Ostrander, and Lynn Schroeder. *Superlearning 2000*, Delacorte Press, 1994

Rose, Colin, and Malcom Nicholl. *Accelerated Learning for the 21st Century*, Dell, 1997.

Zemke, Ron. "Accelerated Learning: Madness with a Method," *Training Magazine,* October 1995.

RELATED WORKS ON LEARNING

Glazer, Steven (ed.). *The Heart of Learning: Spirituality in Education*, Tarcher, 1999.

Langer, Ellen. *The Power of Mindful Learning*, Addison-Wesley, 1997.

Mellander, Klas. *The Power of Learning*, Irwin, 1993.

Vaill, Peter. *Learning As a Way of Being*, Jossey Bass, 1996.

Wenger, Win. *The Einstein Factor: A Proven New Method for Increasing Your Intelligence*, Prima Publishing, 1997.

MENTAL IMAGERY

Bry, Adelaide. *Visualization: Directing the Movies of Your Mind*, Harper & Row, 1978.

Holt, Robert. "Imagery, The Return of the Ostracized," *American Psychologist*, pp. 254-264.

Meier, David. "Imagine That," *Training & Development Journal*, May 1984.

Tower, R.B. "Imagery Training: A Workshop Model," *Imagination, Cognition, and Personality*, 2, 1982-1983.

Wenger, Win. *Beyond Okay*, Psychegenics Press, 1979.

LEARNING STYLES

Armstrong, Thomas. *Multiple Intelligences in the Classroom*, ASCD, 1994.

Armstrong, Thomas. *Seven Kinds of Smart: Identifying and Developing Your Many Intelligences*, Plume, 1993.

Campbell, L & B and Dee Dickinson. *Teaching and Learning Through Multiple Intelligences*, New Horizons for Learning, 1992.

Dunn, R. and K. Dunn. *Teaching Students Through Their Individual Learning Styles: A Practical Approach*, Reston Publishing Co., 1978.

Gardner, Howard. *Frames of Mind: The Theory of Multiple Intelligences*, Basic Books, Harper Collins, 1993.

Gardner, Howard. *Multiple Intelligences: The Theory in Practice*, Basic Books, 1993.

Kolb, David. *Experiential Learning*, Prentice-Hall, 1984.

Lazear, David. *Seven Ways of Teaching: The Artistry of Teaching With Multiple Intelligences*, IRI/Skylight Publications, 1991.

Lazear, David. *Seven Ways of Knowing: Understanding Multiple Intelligences*, IRI/Skylight Publications, 1991.

THE EDUCATION OF CHILDREN

Armstrong, Thomas. *In Their Own Way*, Tarcher, 1987.

Armstrong, Thomas. *Awakening Your Child's Natural Genius*, Tarcher, 1988.

Caine, Geoffrey, Renate Caine, and Sam Crowell. *The Re-Enchantment of Learning: A Manual for Teacher Renewal and Classroom Transformation*, Zephyr Press, 1998.

Caskey, Owen. *Suggestive-Accelerative Learning and Teaching*, Educational Technology Publication, 1980.

Ellis, Susan and Susan Whalen. *Cooperative Learning*, Scholastic Inc., 1990.

Freire, Paulo. *Pedagogy of the Oppressed*, Continuum Publishing, 1970 & 1993.

Fuller, Cheri. *Unlocking Your Child's Learning Potential: How to Equip Kids to Succeed in School and Life*, NavPress, 1994.

Harless, Joe. *The Eden Conspiracy: Educating for Accomplished Citizenship*, Guild V Publications, 1998.

Hunter, Madeline. *Enhancing Teaching*, Macmillan, 1994.

Klein, Peter. *The Everyday Genius*, Great Ocean Publishers, 1988.

McCarthy, Bernice. "Using the 4MAT System to Bring Learning Styles to Schools," *Educational Leadership* 48.2, 1990, pp. 31-37.

McPhee, Doug. *Limitless Learning*, Zephyr Press, 1996.

Pearce, Joseph Chilton. *Evolution's End: Claiming the Potential of Our Intelligence*, Harper Collins, 1992.

Postman, Neil. *The End of Education: Redefining the Value of School*, Vintage Books, 1995.

MUSIC AND LEARNING

Andersen, Ole, Marcy Marsh, and Arthur Harvey. *Learn with the Classics: Using Music to Study Smart at Any Age*, LIND Institute, 1999.

Brewer, Chris and Don Campbell. *Rhythms of Learning: Creative Tools for Developing Lifelong Skills*, Zephyr Press, 1991.

Campbell, Don. *The Mozart Effect*, Avon Books, 1997.

Campbell, Don. *100 Ways to Improve Teaching Using Your Voice and Music*, Zephyr Press, 1992.

Clynes, Manfred (ed.). *Music, Mind and Brain*, Plenum Press, 1982.

Halpern, Steven. *Sound Health*, Harper and Row, 1985.

Halpern, Steven. *Tuning the Human Instrument: An Owner's Manual*, Spectrum Research Institute, 1978.

Merritt, Stephanie. *Mind, Music and Imagery*, Aslan Publishing, 1996.

Webb, Terry Wyler and Douglas Webb. *Accelerated Learning With Music*, Accelerated Learning Systems, 1990.

PICTOGRAMS

Buzan, Tony. *The Mind Map Book: Radiant Thinking*, BBC Books, London, 1993.

Center for Accelerated Learning. *Accelerated Learning Clip Art Book (& software)*, CAL Publishing, 1995. (262) 248-7070.

Claborn, Jo Carol and JoAnn Zerwikh. *The Memory Notebook of Nursing*, Vol I and II. (800) 933-7277.

Margulies, Nancy. *Mapping Inner Space*, Zephyr Press, 1991.

Sibbert, David. *Fundamentals of Graphic Language*, Graphic Guides, 1991.

Sonneman, Milly. *Beyond Words: A Guide to Drawing Out Ideas*, Ten Speed Press, 1997.

Wycoff, Joyce. *Mindmapping*, Berkley Publishing Group, 1991.

Yamamoto, Neal. *Draw 50 Nifty Cartoon Characters*, Lowell House, 1998.

A.L. TECHNIQUES FOR TRAINERS

Bowman, Sharon. *Presenting With Pizzazz*, Bowperson Publishing, 1997.

Bowman, Sharon. *How to Give It So They Get It*, Bowperson Publishing, 1998.

Bowman, Sharon. *Shake, Rattle & Roll*, Bowperson Publishing, 1999.

Coco, Richard and Robert Preziosi. *Accelerating Skill Development, Training & Development Journal*, ASTD, January 1995.

Lawlor, Michael and Peter Handley. *The Creative Trainer: Holistic Facilitation Skills for Accelerated Learning*, McGraw-Hill, 1996.

Lewis, Justus and Moni Lai Storz. *Switch on Your Mind: Accelerated Learning Strategies at Work*, Allen & Unwin, Australia, 1997.

Lohan, Kevin and Alastair Rylatt. *Creating Training Miracles*, Pfeiffer, 1997.

Meier, Thomas, Mark Meier, and David Meier. *The Accelerated Learning CourseBuilder* (a compendium of nine books and associated software), CAL Publishing, 1999.

Miller, Mary and Mary Jeanne Vincent. *Tips for Trainers, Play Breaks*.

Russell, Lou. *The Accelerated Learning Fieldbook*, Jossey-Bass, 1999.

GAMES AND LEARNING EXERCISES

Callahan, *10 Great Games and How to Use Them*, ASTD Infoline.

Epstein, Robert. *Creativity Games for Trainers*, McGraw-Hill, 1996.

Greenblat, C.S. *Designing Games and Simulations*, Sage, 1988.

Insight Software Solutions - Various shareware games - www.smartcode.com/iss.

Leogue, James and Bob Preziosi. *Icebreakers: Warm Up Your Audience*, ASTD Infoline, 1989.

Nilson, Carolyn. *Team Games for Trainers*, McGraw-Hill, 1993.

Peyser, Sandra. *Warm Ups & Wind Downs: 101 Activities for Moving and Motivating Groups*, McLaughlin Publishers.

Rohnke, Karl. *Silver Bullets: A Guide to Adventure Games and Trust Activities*, Kendall/Hunt, 1984.

Silberman, Mel and Karen Lawson. *101 Ways to Make Training Active*, Pfeiffer & Company, 1995.

Sugar, S. *Games That Teach*, Jossey-Bass, 1998.

Thiagarajan, Silvasailam. Games by Thiagi (a series of products), Bloomington, Indiana.

LEARNING AND ORGANIZATIONAL LIFE

Davis, Stan and Jim Botkin. *The Monster Under the Bed,* Simon & Schuster, 1994.

DePorter, Bobbi. *Quantum Business: Achieving Success Through Quantum Learning*, Dell, 1997.

Goleman, Daniel. *Working With Emotional Intelligence.* Bantam Books, 1998.

Kline, Peter and Bernard Saunders. *Ten Steps to a Learning Organization*, Great Ocean Publishers, 1993.

Marshall, Edward. *Transforming the Way We Work: The Power of the Collaborative Workplace*, AMA, 1995.

Senge, Peter & Team. *The Fifth Discipline Fieldbook: Strategies and Tools for Building a Learning Organization*, Doubleday, 1994.

Zohar, Danah. *Rewiring the Corporate Brain*, Berret-Koehler, 1997.

CRITIQUES OF PUBLIC EDUCATION

Gatto, John Taylor. *Dumbing Us Down: The Hidden Curriculum of Compulsory Schooling*, New Society, 1992.

Healy, Jane. *Endangered Minds: Why Children Don't Think and What We Can Do About It,* Simon & Schuster, 1990.

Macedo, Donald. *Literacies of Power: What Americans Are Not Allowed to Know*, Westview Press, 1994.

CRITIQUES OF HIGHER EDUCATION

Bowers, C.A.. *The Culture of Denial*, SUNY Press, 1997.

Saul, John Ralston. *The Unconscious Civilization*, Anansi, Canada, 1995.

Smith, Page. *Killing the Spirit: Higher Education in America*, Penguin Books, 1991.

Orr, David. *Earth in Mind: On Education, Environment, and the Human Prospect,* Island Press, 1994.

CRITIQUES OF TECHNOLOGY-ASSISTED LEARNING

Healy, Jane. *Failure to Connect: How Computers Affect Our Children's Minds for Better and Worse*, Simon & Schuster, 1998.

Oppenheimer, Todd. "The Computer Delusion," *Atlantic Monthly*, July 1997, pp. 45-62.

Postman, Neil. *Technopoly: The Surrender of Culture to Technology*, Vintage, 1993.

Stoll, Clifford. *Silicon Snake Oil*, Anchor Books, 1995.

Strassmann, Paul. *The Squandered Computer: Evaluating the Business Alignment of Information Technologies*, Information Economics Press, 1997.

OTHER BOOKS OF INTEREST

Barzun, Jacques. *Begin Here: The Forgotten Conditions of Teaching and Learning*, Chicago University Press, 1991.

Beniger, James. *The Control Revolution: Technological and Economic Origins of the Information Society*, Harvard University Press, 1986.

Einstein, Elizabeth. *The Printing Revolution in Early Modern Europe*, Cambridge University Press, 1983.

Firestien, Roger. *Leading on the Creative Edge*, Pinon Press, 1996.

Muller, H.J. *The Children of Frankenstein: A Primer on Modern Technology and Human Values*, Indiana University Press, 1970.

Rose, Colin. *Master It Faster*, Accelerated Learning Systems, 1999.

Scheele, Paul. *Natural Brilliance: Move From Feeling Stuck to Achieving Success*, Learning Strategies Corporation, 1997.

Schumacher, E.F. *Small Is Beautiful: Economics as If People Mattered*, Harper & Row, 1973.

Shalin, Leonard. *The Alphabet Versus the Goddess: The Conflict Between Word and Image*, Viking, 1998.

Spretnak, Charlene. *The Resurgence of the Real: Body, Nature, and Place in a Hypermodern World*, Routledge, 1999.

Whyte, David. *The Heart Aroused: Poetry and the Preservation of Soul in Corporate America*, Doubleday, 1994.

MUSIC FOR LEARNING

The possible choices of music for classroom-based and individual learning are endless. Here are just a few suggestions to get you started.

MUSIC TO RELAX THE BODY/MIND
Classical

Pianoforte, Eric Daub (LifeSounds)
Dance of the Blessed Spirits, Gluck (from Orfeo and Euridice)
Relax with the Classics, vol. 2 & 3, (The LIND Institute)
CBS Dinner Classics (French, Italian, and other albums)
Piano Concerto No. 21 (K467), Mozart
Pachelbel's Canon and Other Baroque Favorites, Toronto Chamber Orchestra
Prelude a L'Apres midi d'un Faun, Debussy
The Baroque Lute, Walter Gerwig
Oboe Concertos, Vivaldi
Air on a G String, J.S. Bach

Contemporary

Oceans, Peacock (LifeSounds)
Christofori's Dream, David Lanz
No Blue Thing, Ray Lynch
The Impressionists, Windham Hill Sampler
Piano Solos, Narada Lotus
Silk Road, Kitaro
Velvet Dreams, Kobialka (LifeSounds)
Crystal Silence, Chick Corea
Sunsinger, Paul Winter
A Piece of Heaven, Maia (LifeSounds)

MUSIC TO ENERGIZE THE BODY/MIND
Classical

Eine Kleine Nachtmusik, Mozart
Water Music, Handel
Music for the Royal Fireworks, Handel
Fanfare for the Common Man, Copeland
Gothic Harp, Speero
Fanfares, Mouret
Concerto for Two Pianos (K365), Mozart
Sonata 5 No. 7 in D, Giuseppe Torelli
Trumpet Voluntary, Jeramiah Clark
Suites for Orchestra, Bach
Invitation to the Dance, Weber
Trumpet Concertos, Haydn
Hungarian Dances, Brahms
Triumphal March from Aida, Verdi
Michala Petri Recorder Concertos
Violin, Harp, and Flute Concertos, Telemann
Baroque Music for Panpipes, Zamfir
Dance of the Renaissance, Searles & Yslas (LifeSounds)

Contemporary

Snowflakes are Dancing, Tomita
Deep Breakfast, Ray Lynch
Noveau Flamenco, Ottmar Liebert
Planet Drum (drum music from around the world)
Just Friends, Oliver Jones Trio
Brotherhood, The Gene Harris Quartet
Compact Jazz, Stan Getz
Chase the Clouds Away, Chuck Mangione
Dukes of Dixieland Live
Switched on Bach
Saving the Wildlife, Mannheim Steamroller
Music from *Riverdance*
Earthbeat, Paul Winter
Rondo 2000, Rondo Veneziano
FreshAire, Vols. 2, 3 & 4, Mannheim Steamroller

MUSIC FOR MENTAL IMAGERY AND MEDITATION

Spectrum Suite, Steve Helpern
Natural States, Steve Halpern
Velvet Dreams, Kobialka
Music for Imagining, The LIND Institute
Relax with the Classics, vol. 3, The LIND Institute
Adagio for Strings, Samuel Barber
Tunhuang, Kitaro
Music for Airports, Brian Eno
Silk Road, Kitaro
Inside the Taj Mahal, Paul Horn

MUSIC FOR CONCERT REVIEWS

Christofori's Dream, Lanz
Dance of the Blessed Spirits, Gluck (from Orfeo and Euridice)
Sleepers Awake, J.S. Bach (from Maurice Andre, Back for Trumpet)
Sheep May Safely Graze, J.S. Bach
Brandenberg Concertos Nos. 2 & 5, J.S. Bach
Oceans, Peacock (LifeSounds)

OBTAINING A PERMIT FOR PUBLIC PERFORMANCE

To assure that you are not violating copyright by playing a specific piece of music in the classroom, you can obtain permission from the publisher to use it. For details on this, check with the American Society of Composers, Authors, and Publishers (ASCAP) in New York City at 212-621-6000. Or for answers to frequently asked questions about licensing consult their website: http://www.ascap.com.

Playing copyrighted music in a classroom or training seminar constitutes a *public performance* of the work, requiring that you obtain permission from the owner of the music or his or her representative. There are a couple of exceptions. According to ASCAP, permission is not required for music played or sung as part of a worship service, provided that service is not broadcast by radio or television. Neither is permission required if the performance is part of a face-to-face teaching activity at a nonprofit educational institution.

ASCAP has hundreds of different licensing arrangements covering a wide variety of situations. Not all of them are costly or financially prohibitive. Ask an ASCAP representative to propose a licensing agreement that fits your unique situation and see what happens.

When visiting the ASCAP Web site, you can check out ACE (ASCAP Clearance Express) which contains a searchable database of information on musical compositions, writers, publishers, and recording artists.

Other organizations around the world that could advise you include:

> United Kingdom: Performing Rights Society Ltd.
> South Africa: South African Music Rights Organization Ltd.
> Hong Kong: The Composers and Authors Society of Hong Kong Ltd.
> Australia: Australian Performing Rights Association

SOURCES OF CLASSROOM MUSIC

LifeSounds (1-888-687-4251, music@flite.net) offers high-quality classical and contemporary music that is sold with rights for public performance in a classroom at no additional fee.

In addition, you can contact the following organizations directly. All of these organizations, together with **LifeSounds**, have been associated with the Accelerated Learning movement in the U.S. for years. When you call for their catalogs, explain your situation and ask about their policy regarding public performance of their music tapes and CDs.

Accelerated Learning Systems (GA), 404-446-3852
Barzak Educational Institute (CA), 415-898-0013
The LIND Institute (CA), 800-462-3766 or 415-864-3396
The Mozart Effect Resource Center (CO), 800-721-2177
Steven Halpern's Inner Peace Music (CA), 800-909-0707
Superlearning (NY), 212-279-8430

There are other organizations marketing royalty free music to the training community, but some of it is often shallow, trite, and of low quality according to people musically trained. But don't give up on this avenue. You might be able to find pieces here and there of sufficient quality and appropriateness to work for you.

MUSIC VIDEOS

High quality videos of relaxing nature scenes with music backgrounds can be used for breaks and to accompany some learning activities. Excellent award-winning videos like *Natural States, Desert Visions,* and *Canyon Dreams* can be obtained from **The Entertainer** at 800-609-6111. When you call for a catalog, be sure to ask about their policy regarding classroom use.

MOVIE CLIPS

According to the Federal Copyright Act (Public Law 94-553, Title 17), videocassette clips of copyrighted movies may not be shown publicly without a licence from the copyright owner. This applies equally to for-profit and not-for-profit organizations (including schools). For more information about this, check the Web site of the Motion Picture Licensing Corporation (www.mplc.com/index2.htm). Or you can call them in Los Angeles at (800) 462-8855 to make arrangements for licensing the movies or movie clips you would like to use as part of a training or educational program.

TRAINING SUPPLIES CATALOGS

Occasionally a training design might call for party favors, materials to embellish a theme, or special decorations. If that's the case, here are some organizations that might help you find what you need. Just call for their free catalogs.

Into the Wind Kite Catalog, Boulder, CO: 800-541-0314.

Kipp Brothers, Indianapolis, IN: 800-428-1153.

Oriental Trading Company, Omaha, NE: 800-228-2269

Paradise Products, El Cerrito, CA: 800-227-1092.

Trainers Warehouse, Natick, MA: 800-299-3770.

US Toy Company, Grandview, MO: 816-761-5900.

BOOKS AND RESOURCES ON THE BRAIN AND LEARNING

ASCD, Alexandria, VA: 703-549-9110.

The Brain Store, Del Mar, CA: 800-325-4769.

Herrmann International, Lake Lure, NC: 800-432-4234.

Zephyr Press, Tuscon, AZ: 520-322-5090.

ORGANIZATIONS TEACHING A.L.

The following organizations are friends of the learning revolution and offer workshops in various aspects of A.L. Some offer public workshops, some in-house workshops, and some both. In addition, some specialize in K-12 teacher training, some specialize in corporate training, and some do both. For more information, visit their Web sites, knock on their e-mail doors, or call them for their brochures.

Kat Barclay
Strategic Visions, Inc.
78-1348 Bishop Road
Holualoa, HI 96725
Phone: 808-322-3661
Fax: 808-324-0229
kat.barclay@usa.net

Ivan Barzakov
The Opimalearning Company
885 Olive Avenue, Suite A
Novato, CA 94945
800-672-1717
barzak@optimalearning.com
www. optimalearning.com

Arabella Benson
Fraser McAllan
Masterpiece Corporation
1 Babington Court
Toronto, ON M9A 1J7
Canada
(416) 239-6300
Sponsors of the Center's
Canadian A.L. Workshops

Sharon Bowman
Bowperson Learning Systems
185 Yellowjacket
Glenbrook, NV 89413
702-749-5247
sbowperson@aol.com

Chris Brewer
LifeSounds
160 Seashore Drive
Jupiter, FL 33477
Phone: 561-575-0929
Fax: 561-748-6253
music@flite.net

Marcus Conyers
BrainSMART Inc.
127 W. Fairbank Ave.
Suite 235
Winter Park, FL 32789
Phone: 407-740-8095
Fax: 800-725-5508
marcus@brainsmart.com
www.brainsmart.com

Bobbi DePorter
Learning Forum
1725 South Coast Highway
Oceanside, CA 92054
Phone: 760-722-0072
Fax: 760-722-3507
bdeporter@aol.com

Dee Dickinson
New Horizons for Learning
P.O. Box 15329
Seattle, WA 98115
206-547-7936
building@newhorizons.org

Charlotte Foster
Multivarient Learning
Systems
20 Childs Road
Bernardsville, NJ, 07924
Phone: 908-766-5399
Fax: 908-766-6010
miscal@aol.com

Jeff Haebig
Wellness Quest
1541 7 1/2 Avenue N.E.
Rochester, MN 55906
507-281-3143
welquest@ millcomm.com

Kim Hare & Larry Reynolds
Kaizen Training
Mansion House Farm
Bedmond Rd.
Abbots Langley, HF WD5
0QB, UK
Phone: 01923 262278
Fax: 01923 269680
directors@stables.datanet.co.uk

Gail Heidenhain
Delphin, Inc.
1846 Dorminey Ct.
Lawrenceville, GA 30043
Phone: 770-277-3629
Fax: 770-277-3649
delphin@bellsouth.net

Eric Jensen
Jensen Learning Corporation
P.O. Box 2551
Del Mar, CA 92014
888-638-7246
www.jlcbrain.com

Jenny Maddern
Discovery Learning &
Development
6 Buchanans Wharf North
Ferry Street
Bristol BS1 6HN, UK
Phone: 0117 929 0813
Fax: 0117 929 0813

Nancy Maresh
Maresh Brainworks
3505 23rd. St.
Boulder, CO 80304
303-545-2259
mbrainworks@earthlink.net
www.marishbrainworks.com

Mark McKergow
Mark McKergow Associates
26 Christchurch Road
Cheltenham GL50 2PL, UK
Phone: 01242 511441
Fax: 01242 510941
mark@mckergow.com
http://www.mckergow.com

Doug McPhee
Limitless Learning, Inc.
914 Robley Place
Cardiff, CA 92007-1119
Phone: 760-632-9195
Fax: 760-632-1305
dmcphee@cts.com

Dave Meier
The Center for Accelerated
Learning
1103 Wisconsin Street
Lake Geneva, WI 53147
262-248-7070
alcenter@execpc.com
www.alcenter.com

Claudia Monet
Focus Marketing und mehr
GmbH
Norderstrasse 4
D-24939 Flensburg,
Germany
Phone: 49-461-14 14 8-0
Fax: 49-461-14 14 8-14

Lou Russell
Russell Martin & Associates
6326 Rucker Rd.
Indianapolis, IN 46220
317-475-9311
www.russellmartin.com

Paul Sheele
Learning Strategies Corp.
900 East Wayzata Blvd.
Wayzata, MN 55391-1836
800-735-8273
info@learningstrategies.com
www.learningstrategies.com

Jeannette Vos
The Learning Revolution
International
PO Box 13006
LaJolla, CA 92039-3006
877-575-3276
vos@learning-revolution.com
www.learning-revolution.com

Win Wenger
Project Renaissance
PO Box 332
Gaithersburg, MD 20884-
0332
Phone: 800-649-3800
Fax: 301-515-9030
win@thebestweb.com
http://winwenger.com

LANGUAGE TRAINING IN THE A.L. MODE

Diane Davalos
Expanded Learning
1571 Race Street
Denver, CO 80206
303-333-3445
explearn@aol.com

Karen Houle
University Language Center
1313 Fifth St. S.E., Suite 201
Minneapolis, MN, 55414
612-379-3824
houle@ulanguage.com

University of Houston
Accelerated Learning Program
4800 Calhoun Street
Houston, TX 77204-3901
713-743-1187
Fax: 713-743-1203
shsawyer @bayou.uh.edu

Alison Miller
Pacific Language Center
P.O. Box 1282
Anacortes, WA 98221
360-299-9389
indigo@fidalgo.net

Pearl Nitsche
Super Language Learning
Florianigasse 55
A-1080, Vienna, Austria
43-1-408-4184
Fax: 43-1-403-6602
pearl@ping.at

WEB SITES

www.alcenter.com
A source of A.L. products and services for training professionals containing a message board, downloadable demos, and monthly tips for speeding and enhancing learning.

www.dana.org
Has links to brain research and the downloadable newsletter *Brain Work*.

www.newhorizons.org
A large website of resources on leading-edge K-12 learning, adult learning, brain-based learning, and much more.

www.superlearning.com
A source of books, articles, music, audiotape programs, and other accelerated learning resources.

RESOURCES FROM THE CENTER FOR ACCELERATED LEARNING

262-248-7070 - alcenter@execpc.com - www.alcenter.com

The Accelerated Learning CourseBuilder. A large kit of books and resources containing over 500 A.L. activities plus an integrated system (in both manual and computerized form) for designing learning programs quickly.

Quiz Show. Computerized games (jeopardy-type and tic-tac-toe) for learning and review that allow you to enter question sets quickly and play with partners or teams. A demo can be downloaded from the website.

Accelerated Learning Clip Art. A manual and software collection of hand-drawn images that can be used to create course maps, presentation graphics, and other learning aids.

INTERNATIONAL CONFERENCES ON ACCELERATED LEARNING

The United States

> The International Alliance for Learning
> 1040 South Coast Highway
> Encinitas, CA 92024
> 800-426-2989
> info@ialearn.org
> www.ialearn.org

England

> S.E.A.L.
> (Society for Effective Affective Learning)
> P.O. Box 2246
> Bath, BA1 2YR, UK
> Phone: 44-1225-466244
> Fax: 44-1225-444024

Germany

> D.G.S.L.
> (The German Society for Suggestopedic
> Teaching and Learning)
> Horlkofener Str. 2
> D-85457 Worth, Germany
> Phone: 08123-991000
> Fax: 08123-991001
> dgsl@compuserve.com
> http://ourworld.compuserve.com/homepages/dgsl/

A Special Thanks to:

Peter Janzen of *Peter S. Janzen Art & Design* in Fontana, Wisconsin for providing all the artwork in this book.

Tom Meier of *Center for Accelerated Learning* for gathering and compiling many of the examples used in this book.

Richard Narrramore of *McGraw-Hill* who initially suggested that this book be written and saw it through to completion.

Lyn Palombi of *Marlin Printing & Graphics* in Waukesha, Wisconsin, for the design and layout of this book.

About the Author:

Dave Meier is director of the Center for Accelerated Learning in Lake Geneva, Wisconsin, an organization he founded in 1980. Since then, through public and in-house workshops in North America and overseas, he has prepared more corporate training professionals in accelerated learning than any other person worldwide.

INDEX

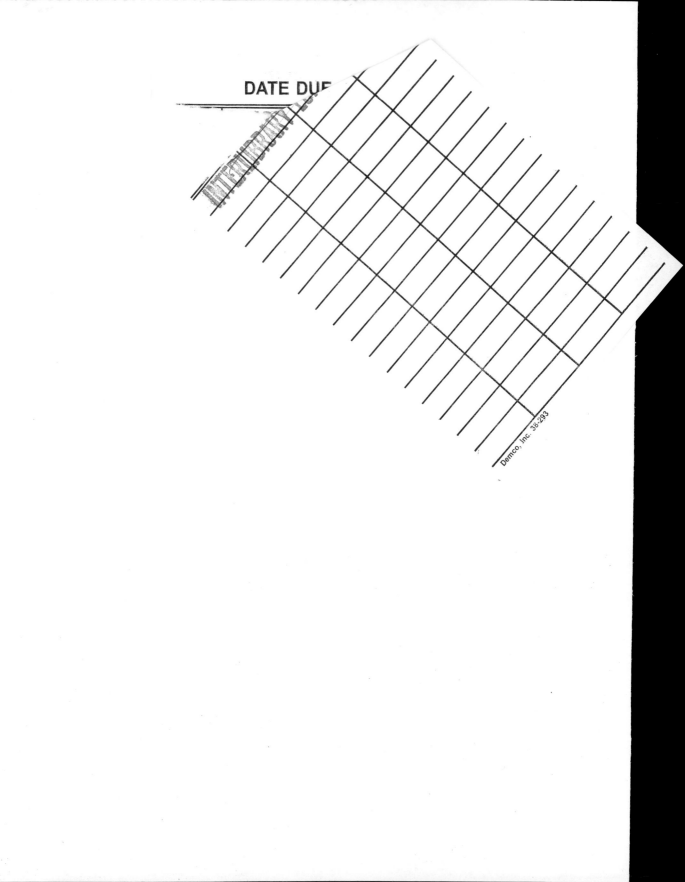

DATE DUE

Demco, Inc. 38-293